## Also by Steve Dugan

*The Nine Words: A Story of Faith,
Love & Perseverance*

*Great News From God!*

# JIMMY CARTER
## & FRIENDS

### STEVE DUGAN

WESTBOW
PRESS®
A DIVISION OF THOMAS NELSON
& ZONDERVAN

WestBow Press books may be ordered through booksellers or by contacting:

WestBow Press
A Division of Thomas Nelson & Zondervan
1663 Liberty Drive
Bloomington, IN 47403
www.westbowpress.com
844-714-3454

ISBN: 979-8-3850-1928-1 (sc)
ISBN: 979-8-3850-1929-8 (e)

Library of Congress Control Number: 2024903487

Print information available on the last page.

WestBow Press rev. date: 03/18/2024

# CONTENTS

**Part Two - Jack Brinkley**

# DEDICATION

---

**To Julie,**

**The very greatest person**

**God ever put in my life.**

# FOREWORD

I met both Jimmy Carter and Jack Brinkley on the same occasion in 1966, when I was a sophomore in high school. I was very blessed by God to get to work for and become friends with both of them.

After Jack Brinkley died and Jimmy Carter went into hospice care, I realized it was important to me to preserve some of my memories of them. The purpose of this book is not to describe what they did. It is to show their human side.

If you have ever wondered what Jimmy Carter was like "behind the scenes" or what it was like to work for a member of Congress, I hope you will enjoy the stories in this book. These are the memories that I like to share with my family and friends.

Steve Dugan
Mobile, Alabama
January 14, 2024

# CHAPTER 1

## How I Met Jimmy Carter

In February of 1966, when I was a sophomore in high school, I went with some friends to an Affirmation Vietnam Rally at Atlanta Stadium in Atlanta. It was designed as a way for people to show support for our soldiers in Vietnam. I remember that rally very well. It was cold and rainy. There were so few people there that we were all able to sit in the small second deck of the stadium, called the Club Section, which offered some protection from the weather.

The small crowd depressed me. On the way home, I decided to try to organize an Affirmation Vietnam Rally at Fort Valley High School. I knew that if we held it in the school's large basketball gym, we would have a packed crowd and a lot better atmosphere to support our soldiers than what I had witnessed in Atlanta.

I can't remember the details of how this was arranged, but we did hold an Affirmation Vietnam Rally in the Fort Valley High School gym on Saturday night, March 5, 1966. It was raining very hard outside, but the basketball gym was full of very patriotic and enthusiastic people.

1966 was an election year in Georgia. Some politicians running for congressional and state wide offices came to Fort Valley and spoke at that rally. They were all nice to me.

One of them was State Representative Jack T. Brinkley of Columbus. I would later work for him as his Legislative Assistant when he was a Member of Congress and practice law with him after he retired from politics.

Since I had been selected to be the master of ceremonies for the rally, I had the opportunity to meet informally with the visiting politicians before the rally started in a classroom which the school had set aside for that purpose. That was when I met Jimmy Carter for the first time. We really hit it off talking in that room before the rally started. I had not even heard of him before that night.

During that rally, I introduced Jimmy Carter to the big crowd. He started his remarks by saying, "I just met Steve Dugan. He promised to support me in my campaign this year, and I promised to support him later on when he runs for President." The Fort Valley crowd got a big kick out of that.

I don't remember anything else about that night. But a few days later I received the following letter from Jimmy Carter.

Plains, Georgia

March 8, 1966

Honorable Steve Dugan

Fort Valley, Georgia

Dear Steve:

It was a real pleasure for me to come to Fort Valley last week to participate in your fine program and to meet a future President. I told my family when I returned home that I had never met a young man who was more interesting and impressive than you.

I hope that you are sincere in wishing to pursue a career in politics. I have mixed feelings about whether it is man's lowest or highest calling, and I believe it can be either, depending on the candidate. If one is eager to use his own dynamic personality and talents for his own personal gain in income or in personal glory or publicity, then it can be the lowest calling. But if a genuine concern for people whom he represents causes him to become totally immersed in their problems, hopes, dreams and aspirations so that he can represent their best interests even when they conflict with his own, then it can be a high calling. In the latter case there is no excuse for hard, detailed and thankless work, while on the other hand a few bright, meaningless statements to the press can serve the purpose. Perhaps this is all an over-simplification, but not far from an accurate analysis.

I want your help this year in my campaign. We can learn together. I look forward to seeing you when I come to Fort Valley. Right now I am trying to consolidate support in Columbus to avoid a Democratic opponent from there.

Sincerely,

Jimmy

He was a 41 year old graduate of the Naval Academy who had played a leading role in creating America's nuclear submarine program and then became a State Senator. But, that did not keep him from becoming a true friend to a 15 year old high school sophomore. He treated me with the same level of respect that he treated adults. That is indicative of the fact that he did not see people as members of an age group, race, gender or anything else. He treated people as individuals.

The other politicians I met that night were also nice to me, but only Jimmy Carter took the time to write me a letter after meeting me at that rally. He pushed himself harder to achieve his goals than any other person I ever knew.

# CHAPTER 2

## He Cared Enough To Come

One day not long after Jimmy Carter wrote me that letter, I was sitting in a classroom at Fort Valley High School. Somebody from the school office came into the room and told my teacher that I should report to the superintendent's office.

When I walked into the superintendent's office, there was Jimmy Carter. He asked me to sit down and then he closed the door.

He told me that he had decided to run for Governor instead of for Congress, as he had been doing. When I asked him why, he told me that the man he had been running for Congress against, Congressman Bo Callaway, had decided to run for Governor.

I told him I didn't understand his decision.

Now that Callaway was giving up his seat in Congress to run for Governor, Carter would have an excellent chance to be elected to Congress. On the other hand, there were already several well known and well financed candidates for the Democratic nomination for Governor that year. So, Carter would be a huge underdog if he ran for Governor.

I remember Jimmy Carter sternly looking me in the eyes. "You don't understand," he said, "I want to beat Bo Callaway."

Bo Callaway was a good man and a very rich Republican. I got the impression that Jimmy Carter was determined to run against Callaway, because Carter did not think that Callaway understood the regular people of Georgia nearly as well as he did.

I think Carter gave me some literature to give out about his campaign. We had a good talk, but that was well over half a century ago, and I don't remember anything else that was said.

Most politicians would have made the choice to do what was in their best interest and get elected to Congress. Carter did not think that way. He had his goal set on beating Callaway, and he wasn't going to change his goal.

Jimmy Carter was a highly competitive man. He was always driven to achieve very specific and difficult goals. A lot of people who didn't really know him could not see this because of his soft voice and big smile.

The biggest thing I remember about that day was simply the fact that Jimmy Carter had cared enough about me to come to my high school, get me out of class, and talk with me. I'm sure he had a lot of more important things to do and places to go, and I'm sure he was very tired.

Nonetheless, Carter had written me that he was going to stop and see me when he passed through Fort Valley, and it was important to him to keep his word. With all that was on his mind, he did not forget about an unimportant high school sophomore to whom he had made a promise. I don't know if any other politician would have done that.

# CHAPTER 3

## The Call That Changed My Life

After the 1965-1966 school year ended, many young people in Fort Valley got summer jobs working in the peach packing sheds on the outskirts of town. I had a job loading peaches into shipping boxes. I didn't like it, but it was a job.

One night, I got a call at the peach shed. When I got into the office and picked up the phone, what I heard was a total surprise to me.

"Hello, Steve," the voice said. "This is Jimmy Carter. Would you like to come to Atlanta and work for me in my state headquarters this summer?"

"Yes, sir," I said. "I sure would."

"Well," he replied, "I'll talk with your parents and see if they'll let you do it."

It was the only call I ever got at that peach shed.

That night, when I got home, Jimmy Carter had already talked with Momma and Daddy. He had promised them that he would give me a room right next to his and Miss Rosalynn's room in the Dinkler Plaza Hotel in downtown Atlanta, and that he would keep an eye on me.

The next Sunday, my Daddy drove me the one hundred miles from Fort Valley to Atlanta and dropped me off with Mr. Bob Short. He was Jimmy Carter's campaign manager that year. Mr. Short was a very smart and good man.

When Jimmy Carter had written me after that rally in Fort Valley and come to see me at Fort Valley High School a few days later, he had said he wanted me to work for him in his campaign. Those are very easy words that many politicians just say and then forget.

Jimmy Carter was different. I learned that very quickly. He must have gone to a lot of trouble just to find out where I was working and how to get the phone number where I could be reached.

I wish I had asked him how and why he did those things, but now I will never know. I just know that he changed my life when he called me.

# CHAPTER 4

## The Press Club

On my first full day of working for him at his headquarters in Atlanta in early June of 1966, Jimmy Carter asked me to accompany him to the Atlanta Press Club, which had invited him to make a speech. This was an important occasion, because Carter was still unknown by many people in the Atlanta media.

When we got to the room in which he was to speak to these influential journalists, Jimmy Carter told me to stay just outside the door. He told me to stand there when the reporters filed out of the meeting and listen to what they said about him as they were leaving.

I did just what he asked me to do. After they had all left, Jimmy Carter and I got back in the car and sat down. He looked at me with interest and said, "What did they say?"

For some reason, I developed the habit of calling him "Governor," because I had to call him something. I didn't think I should call him "Jimmy," and I never once did. But, calling him "Mr. Carter" would have been too formal. I could have called him "Senator," because he was a State Senator at the time.

However, I decided to call him "Governor" instead, because that was the office he was working so hard to obtain. I wanted to show him that I had unshakeable confidence in him, even on tough days for the campaign.

"Well, Governor," I answered, "They said they couldn't understand you."

Hearing that would have made a lot of politicians angry or defensive. That was not Jimmy Carter's way. He had been confronted with a lot of obstacles in his life. His analytical side showed a lot more than his emotional side. To him, it was a simple problem. If the people in the Atlanta media had trouble understanding his thick South Georgia accent, he would fix the problem.

When we got back to the headquarters, he called WSB TV. They had a very popular anchorman who everybody in Atlanta could understand perfectly. Jimmy Carter asked if he could come to the TV station one night a week and be taught how to speak more clearly by this anchorman. It took a lot of humility to do that. But, Jimmy Carter saw it as just another step towards improving his chances to be elected. He never let pride stand between him and his goal.

# CHAPTER 5

## The Fan and The Son

During the 1966 campaign, there used to be meetings in the state headquarters late at night after Jimmy Carter came back from wherever he had been campaigning that day. I would sit in at these meetings, at which Carter and a small group of his key supporters would discuss the campaign.

One issue that got brought up was Carter's image. Some advisors were concerned that he might come across as too rural.

Today, the very same things that some of his friends were concerned about back in 1966 are considered positive parts of his authenticity. Just as Abraham Lincoln rose from a log cabin to become President, Jimmy Carter rose from a peanut farm.

At the time, however, the small group of people sitting in the headquarters late at night discussing the campaign never even thought of the possibility that one day Jimmy Carter would be elected President of The United States and win the Nobel Peace Prize. The goal of these people was only to do everything possible to get him elected Governor of Georgia.

Jimmy Carter's family was a collection of very interesting and hard working people. One of my favorites was Jimmy Carter's mother, who I always called Miss Lillian.

One time, when I went to spend the weekend with the Carters, I stayed with Miss Lillian at her small house in the country outside of Plains. There was a little pond in front of it, where she liked to fish.

Among many other things, Miss Lillian was a big wrestling fan. There used to be televised wrestling matches broadcast from Columbus, Georgia one night every week. Miss Lillian used to attend, and she liked to sit on the front row.

Some advisors thought this could be damaging to Jimmy Carter's image. So, they thought it would be wise if Miss Lillian did not go to any more wrestling matches until after the election.

They must not have understood what a strong minded woman Miss Lillian was and what a devoted son Jimmy Carter was. I was told that a compromise was reached. Miss Lillian could keep going to the wrestling matches, but she would be asked to wear a disguise.

That 1966 campaign was fifty-seven years ago, and my memory is not as good as I wish it were. So, I checked on the internet to verify that my memory that there had been a strong connection between Miss Lillian and wrestling was correct. Here is what I discovered.

She was quoted as saying that the more brutal wrestling matches were, the more she liked them. She also said that the wrestlers were nice young men with good physiques and beautiful bodies. I even saw a famous picture of Jimmy Carter with Miss Lillian's favorite wrestler, "Mr. Wrestling II."

There is also a picture of Miss Lillian with "Mr. Wrestling II." Once, when her son was President, Miss Lillian invited "Mr. Wrestling II" to visit her at her house outside Plains. The Secret Service brought him. One thing that worried The Secret Service was that "Mr. Wrestling II" wore his trademark white mask, which he would not take off under any circumstances.

When "Mr. Wrestling II" and the Secret Service agents bringing him got to Miss Lillian's house, the agents felt consternation over the fact that "Mr. Wrestling II" would not remove his mask. However, much to the agents' chagrin, that did not bother Miss Lillian.

Before the agents knew it, Miss Lillian had invited "Mr. Wrestling II" into her house and closed the door. "Mr. Wrestling II" said she asked him if his wife thought he was cute.

"Mr. Wrestling II" replied that since his wife had married him, he assumed that she thought he was cute. He said that Miss Lillian quickly responded by saying, "Oh, that's lovely."

"Mr. Wrestling II" was reportedly invited to Jimmy Carter's Presidential inauguration. When he showed up in his mask, the Secret Service agents said he would have to either remove his mask or leave. So, being true to the wrestlers' code, "Mr. Wrestling II" left.

President Jimmy Carter appointed a man who was a leading Georgia wrestling promoter and a member of a Wrestling Hall of Fame to the National Council for the Arts. A list of other wrestling Hall of Famers includes "Mr. Wrestling II" and Abraham Lincoln, who loved wrestling and excelled at it.

So, I feel better about my memory when it comes to Miss Lillian being such a big wrestling fan. Of course, Miss Lillian was a lot more than that.

When she was 28, Miss Lillian was the midwife who delivered her future daughter-in-law, Rosalynn Smith. When she was 68, she joined The Peace Corps and served two years in India. She was very smart and knew how to get the most favorable coverage for her son out of every encounter she had with the media.

Most importantly, she was kind to people from all walks of life, including me. If you want to know what the Carters were really like, you can start with the fact that they were genuine and caring.

# CHAPTER 6

## Miss Rosalynn Speaks Her Mind

In 1966, there were six candidates for the Democratic Party's nomination for Governor of Georgia. The leading candidate was former Governor Ellis Arnall of Newnan.

Arnall had been elected to the Georgia House of Representatives at age 25. He was then elected Speaker Pro Tempore, the second highest office in that body. When he was 31, he was appointed by the Governor to become the Attorney General of Georgia. In 1942, he defeated the powerful populist Eugene Talmadge to become the youngest Governor in the United States.

Arnall successfully argued major cases for the State of Georgia before The United States Supreme

Court. He got the poll tax repealed, got a new state constitution ratified, and retired the state's debt, among many other accomplishments.

Indicative of his high character, he reasoned that if 18 year olds were old enough to fight and die in war for their country, they were old enough to vote. Therefore, he succeeded in making Georgia the first state to allow 18 year olds to vote. The United States would not pass the 26th amendment to the United States Constitution allowing 18 year olds to vote nationwide for 20 more years.

Arnall was a proponent of civil rights and argued that African Americans should be able to vote in the Democratic Party's primary elections. These primaries decided all office holders in Georgia, since there was not a viable Republican Party in the state at the time.

Arnall's reforms won him acclaim in the national press. He served President Truman as Director of The Office of Price Stabilization. After that, Truman offered Arnall the position of Solicitor General of the United States, but Arnall turned it down to return to private law practice. He founded one of Atlanta's premier law firms and became a multimillionaire. Today, there is a statue of him on the state capitol grounds.

In 1948, Ellis Arnall was unanimously elected in Hollywood as President of The Society of Independent Motion Picture Producers. He was hosted and sponsored by David O. Selznick, Samuel Goldwyn, and Walt Disney, with whom Arnall became close personal friends. On top of everything else, Arnall was a bestselling author.

Ellis Arnall was a man of high character, progressive ideals, and superior intellect. In addition, he was a gifted politician and a tough opponent. Yet, it was Arnall whom Jimmy Carter would have to beat to become the Democratic Party's nominee for Governor of Georgia in 1966.

All of us working in the Carter campaign had to try to figure out the most effective way to persuade moderate and liberal voters to choose Jimmy Carter instead of Ellis Arnall. It was not an easy thing to do.

As Carter's Teenage Campaign Manager, one of my jobs was to make talks to groups of young people around the state. On one such occasion, I was invited to make a talk to a group of young people and some of their parents in one of the most affluent and liberal neighborhoods in Atlanta. That was prime Arnall country.

I believed in being totally honest in my talks. Besides being what I thought was the right thing to do, being totally honest in these talks also seemed like the smart thing to do. It gained me some credibility with audiences who were predisposed to support Arnall and to be suspicious of Carter.

During this talk at a home in an affluent section of Atlanta, my argument was that, while Arnall was probably smarter than Carter, Carter was also very smart and was much more in touch with the views of average Georgians than Arnall. I also argued that Carter, who was seen as a moderate, could beat the conservative Republican Bo Callaway in the general election, while Arnall would have a much harder time doing so. I thought it was a good talk, and it seemed to make some of the young Arnall supporters in the small audience at least think about switching their support to Carter.

Somehow, Norman Shavin, a very prominent author whose column appeared every morning on the Atlanta Constitution editorial page, heard of my remarks. The headline of his column the next morning was something like "Carter Spokesman Admits Arnall is Smarter."

I found out about this in a very memorable way. Very early the next morning, I was in the headquarters when Miss Rosalynn came through the door. She walked up to me with the morning paper in her hand. She did not seem happy.

"Don't let me hear that you said anybody is smarter than Jimmy ever again!" she said emphatically. Then, she left the room.

Miss Rosalynn was an extremely smart woman and a very major part of everything Jimmy Carter ever accomplished. More than any other husband and wife team in political history, they were equal partners in Jimmy Carter's career. She was not the type of political wife who just stood up and smiled, when she was introduced before her husband made a speech.

Jimmy Carter listened to Miss Rosalynn more than he listened to anybody else. That's why she participated in cabinet meetings when Jimmy Carter was President.

She always treated me like a member of the Carter family before and after that morning. I still have some wonderful letters she wrote to me over many years.

But, more than anything else, she was totally devoted to Jimmy Carter. After that conversation, I never said anybody was smarter than Jimmy Carter again.

As it turned out, Miss Rosalynn was right. As outstanding a man as Ellis Arnall was, he never got elected President of the United States, won the Nobel Prize, or eradicated a horrible disease from the face of the earth. Jimmy Carter really was smarter.

Rosalynn Carter never said anything about this speech to me again, and Jimmy Carter never said anything about it to me at all. Furthermore, nobody told me what I could or could not say or write while communicating with people on behalf of Jimmy Carter.

I have often said that I think Miss Rosalynn may have been even more competitive than Jimmy Carter. I admired her for her passion and for her excruciatingly hard work. You could see the fire in her eyes.

Most of all, I appreciated how kind she was to me. In her capacity as First Lady, her special goal was to help people with mental illnesses and take away the stigma associated with having them.

Many years after Jimmy Carter's term as President was over, I had severe anxiety and depression. When Jimmy and Rosalynn Carter heard about it, they went to extraordinary lengths to help and encourage me. That is one reason that I wanted to write this book.

# CHAPTER 7

## On The Trail With Jimmy Carter

I don't remember how this came about or any more details about it, but this story has stuck with me. One afternoon in the summer of 1966, I was with Jimmy Carter campaigning in a small town in south Georgia.

Like most towns that were county seats, this town had a court square, with streets of shops and businesses facing the county courthouse from all four directions. This area was called "downtown."

After we parked and got out of the car, Jimmy Carter and I started walking around the court square. He looked every person he met right in the eyes, introduced himself, shook the person's hand, and asked what the person's name was. Then, he would continue to look into that person's eyes as he listened carefully to whatever the person wanted to tell him. After he finished talking with a person, I would give that person a campaign brochure.

Jimmy Carter was an excellent listener, and that was very important. When he introduced himself to a person, he would always say, "Hello. I'm Jimmy Carter, and I'm running for Governor."

On the day this story occurred, he wore khaki pants with a white shirt and a necktie. He had a way of rolling his shirt sleeves up so the bottom half of his forearms were uncovered. He always wore a wristwatch with the face of the watch on the bottom of his wrist. He would have to flip his wrist over to look at his watch.

We went from business to business. Then, we got to a beauty parlor. I did not want to go inside, but Jimmy Carter didn't give it a thought. He just opened the door, and in we went.

I still vividly remember seeing a long row of women sitting under those big hair dryers and reading magazines. Their hair was rolled up in curlers. I did not think it was a very attractive sight.

They didn't look up because they couldn't hear anything under those loud hair dryers. This was not a problem for Jimmy Carter. He just knocked on the top of those hard hair dryers like he was knocking on their front door.

The women under the hair dryers looked a little bothered when they heard that knocking above their heads. But when they saw Jimmy Carter, they would put down their magazine, remove the hair dryer from their heads, and smile.

He told each of these women the same thing he told the people he met on the street. But, there was one difference. After he finished his brief visit with one of these women, Jimmy Carter would bend down and kiss her on the cheek. Then, I would give her a brochure.

When we left the beauty parlor and got back on the sidewalk. I said, "Governor, how could you kiss all those women in those awful curlers?"

He looked at me and laughed. He said, "Don't worry. If I win the nomination, they'll tell all their friends that I kissed them. And, if I get elected Governor, it's no telling what they'll say!"

If it had been me campaigning in his place, I would not have had the self-confidence he projected to every person he met. I wouldn't have been relaxed or enjoyed this type of campaigning, either. But, I got the impression that Jimmy Carter really enjoyed campaigning like this. It came naturally to him, and he was confident in his ability to connect with people.

I believe the only reason Jimmy Carter did not get elected Governor in 1966 was that he didn't have the time to meet enough people one-on-one. It's the most time consuming way to campaign, but it was very effective for him.

The day after he lost his bid to become Governor in 1966, he started working on his 1970 campaign. He never wasted a day.

He was confident that if he pushed himself as hard as he could and kept campaigning non-stop all over Georgia for the next four years, he would be elected Governor in 1970 no matter who ran against him. And, he was right.

There was nobody else like Jimmy Carter when it came to genuinely caring for people's needs. I saw that as I followed him around in that small town. The people he met saw it, too. Later, the whole world would see it in the things he did both as President and after he was President.

# CHAPTER 8

## Bumps Along The Way

Today, most candidates decide one or two years in advance before they run for a statewide or national office. This gives them plenty of time to line up the financing they need, hire a staff, and prepare in other important ways, too.

But in 1966, Jimmy Carter only decided to run for Governor in mid-March. Until then, he had been running a low budget campaign for the U.S. Congress.

Since the Democratic primary election was in September, Carter only had a little over five full months to organize his campaign, raise the money he needed for even a modest effort, and get his name known across the Georgia's 159 counties.

When Jimmy Carter wrote me after we met at that rally at the Fort Valley High School gym, he said that we could "learn together." He was not exaggerating. All of us working in the campaign did the best we could, but we made plenty of mistakes as we went along.

One involved the first "telephone pole posters" the campaign ordered. These are large posters designed to be nailed to telephone poles all over the state.

All the candidates had them. One afternoon in 1966, I was driving down an empty country road when I saw a man high up on a ladder nailing his campaign poster to a telephone pole.

It was Lester Maddox, who won the election that year and became Governor of Georgia. Maddox had mastered the art of using "telephone pole posters." By using a long ladder he carried on his truck, he could nail his posters so high on the telephone poles that it was very hard for anybody to tear them down.

He also understood the importance of name recognition. From top to bottom, his posters simply read, "Maddox! Maddox! Maddox! Maddox! Maddox!" His "telephone pole poster" plan was extremely effective.

Since Jimmy Carter did not have time to raise much money for his campaign, every dollar mattered. And "telephone pole posters" were very expensive.

I remember a lot of conversations within the campaign about what kind of "telephone pole posters" to buy. The people who made the decision decided to order slick white posters with a big blue picture of Jimmy Carter's face and "Jimmy Carter for Governor" printed in orange below the picture.

The day the posters arrived, we were all very excited. But, when we looked at one, we realized the orange lettering was pretty hard to read and not very attractive.

The campaign had chosen the orange coloring for one reason. The company that made the posters promised they would glow in the dark at night as cars' headlights hit them.

Unfortunately, we found out that the orange lettering would fade away the first time it rained. The posters were a complete bust. We envisioned Jimmy Carter's entire political career fading away with the orange lettering on those posters.

Another depressing mistake was the big Augusta breakfast disaster. The campaign had spent a lot of money renting a large room in an Augusta hotel, hiring a company to prepare a big breakfast for 200 or so guests, printing invitations, and mailing them.

This was the biggest and most expensive undertaking by the campaign so far. It was to the fledgling Carter campaign what the first flight into space had been to the space program.

Very early on the morning of this big event, I watched a confident and business-like Jimmy Carter walk out of the headquarters with a smiling Miss Rosalynn and their youngest son, Jeff. They were leaving for the breakfast in Augusta.

Jeff was really looking forward to that big breakfast in Augusta. He told me that he was going to eat all the food set out for any people who did not show up.

That afternoon, the Carters returned from their trip to Augusta and walked into to the headquarters. Jimmy Carter had a frustrated look on his face. Miss Rosalynn looked angry. But, Jeff had a big smile as he walked towards me.

"What happened?" I asked him.

"Well," he said triumphantly, "I just had two hundred glasses of orange juice!"

It turned out that the invitations had the wrong date on them. When the Carters got there, nobody showed up.

But, the food had already been prepared and the orange juice had already been placed by the plates. By the time the mistake on the invitations had been discovered, it was too late to do anything about it.

Jeff had hit the jackpot. There was nothing you could do at a time like that but laugh and trust God to keep the campaign going.

# CHAPTER 9

## Jeff and Shoney's

The Carters had three sons. Jack turned 19 during the 1966 campaign, and Chip was my age, 16. Jeff, with whom I became close friends, was 14.

I really liked Jeff. He was completely unpretentious and had a great sense of humor.

Jeff and I would eat our two meals a day at the Shoney's Big Boy located right beside the Dinkler Plaza Hotel on Forsyth Street in downtown Atlanta. We never had any money to spare, so we devised what we thought was a clever trick to get our meals.

One of us would order the half pound of ground round and a glass of ice tea with extra lemons. The other one would just ask for a glass of water.

When the waitress brought the food, the one of us who had asked for just a glass of water would take the extra lemons that came with the other person's ice tea, combine them with sugar from the large sugar dispenser on the table, and thereby turn the free glass of water into lemonade.

Then, we would split the half pound of ground round. Since that was often all we could afford, we did not always have any money to leave as a tip.

By the end of the summer, the waitresses were on to us. We would have to wait a long time before a waitress would come to our table. While we were waiting, Jeff would go to an unoccupied table and unscrew the top of the big sugar dispenser on that table.

Then, we would wait for people to come sit at the table and attempt to pour some sugar into their coffee. Unfortunately for them, the top of the sugar dispenser would come completely off and the entire contents of the sugar dispenser would spill all over the unsuspecting diners and their table.

I am ashamed to say that we thought this was hilarious. So, Jeff and I sort of wore out our welcome at Shoney's by the time the campaign was over. We were lucky the waitresses had a sense of humor and kept waiting on us at all.

After the campaign, on March 6, 1967, Jeff wrote me a letter which I still have. In it he reminisced about our experiences at that Shoney's Big Boy restaurant during the campaign. He included a poem that he said could be sung to the tune of "Downtown" about our experiences ordering "Ground Round" twice a day at Shoney's. We had a good time together.

# CHAPTER 10

## My Job In The Campaign

I was always what you would call a nerd. I wasn't coordinated enough to be good at sports. So, I adopted politics as my substitute. I approached politics the way other kids approached baseball. I just wanted to get on a good team and play.

I had only met Jimmy Carter two times before he offered me a job, so I didn't really know him. He didn't really know me, either. I guess we both had a good instinctive feeling about each other.

Jimmy Carter had started his campaign late, and he didn't have a lot of money to spend on staff. If he had, I'm sure he would have hired somebody better than me.

My job was to be his Teenage Campaign Manager. It was a great opportunity for me. But, if the Carter campaign had been a baseball team, I would have been a lot more like the bat boy than the starting pitcher.

I don't really remember what I got paid. It was probably the same amount I would have made working at that peach shed. The only things I remember getting for sure were a room in the hotel which I shared with another young staff member and some money for food and transportation back and forth from Atlanta to Fort Valley on the weekends.

As the campaign plowed on through the summer, Jimmy Carter and I got to know each other better. As time went on, my respect for him grew, and I believe his confidence in me grew, too.

As Jimmy Carter's Teenage Campaign Manager, my goal was to build up an ever increasing group of teenagers around the state who would tell their friends and their parents about how much they liked Carter. I developed a plan to accomplish this goal, and I worked very hard at it.

I prepared a letter to send to any Georgia teenagers whose names and addresses I could get. With this letter, I included a form I prepared on which they could give me the names and addresses of ten of their friends. When they filled out these forms and mailed them back to me, I immediately sent all their friends the same letter and materials I had sent them.

I also wrote a weekly "Teenagers For Carter Newsletter." I sent it to every teenager whose name and address I had. It kept them informed about how the campaign was doing and where Carter would be campaigning the next week.

Mail was delivered to the headquarters several times every day. I was constantly busy sending out the letter, form and newsletter to every new teenager whose name and address I received.

After a few weeks, I was receiving and sending out a lot of mail every day. On many days, I would not even go to bed. I would just go to my room at 6:00 AM, take a shower, change clothes and go back to my desk.

While he was on the campaign trail, Jimmy Carter started meeting people who said their children were in "Teenagers For Carter." I think that made Carter think I was creating some good enthusiasm for him.

I wasn't the only young person to whom Jimmy Carter took an instinctive liking and asked to join his campaign. I was with Carter in the headquarters one day when a State Senator from Albany came in and introduced Carter to another young man.

This young man had heard Carter give a speech at the Albany Elks Club. They had talked after that speech and hit it off just like Carter and I had when we first met.

Jimmy Carter introduced me to that young man. Carter told me that he was going to join the campaign as Youth Coordinator and suggested we share the room in which I had been staying.

That young man's name was Hamilton Jordan. He was six years older than I was. Hamilton would go on to work with Carter in the highest positions until the day Carter finished his term as President.

Hamilton and I became very close friends. He had a great sense of humor, and I can see him rolling his eyes and hear him laughing as I write this. We believed in Jimmy Carter, we worked hard, and we had a lot of fun.

Carter liked my enthusiasm, and he had heard me speak at the rally in Fort Valley back in March. So, he decided to let me introduce him at Sunday afternoon meetings to which he invited his campaign managers from all over Georgia.

I would always finish my introduction of him by saying the following. "Now, friends, I have the honor to introduce to you the man who will make our roads safer, our schools better, our grass greener, and our sky bluer. Here he is, the next Governor of the great, sovereign and Southern state of Georgia, 'The Plain Man's Man From Plains,' Jimmy Carter!"

Jimmy Carter would have just finished a grueling week on the campaign trail when I introduced him and his eyes would be bloodshot from exhaustion. But, I can still see the big happy grin he would always have on his face after he heard that introduction. He would thank me as the crowd stood up and cheered for him. At times like that, I knew that God had blessed me by letting me get to know such a special friend.

# CHAPTER 11

## An End And A Beginning

The 1966 Georgia Democratic Party primary election was held on Tuesday, September 13. The law in Georgia provided that, if no candidate got a majority of the votes, the top two finishers would meet in a runoff several weeks later.

There were six candidates for the Democratic nomination for Governor. Jimmy Carter's goal was to be one of the top two finishers and thus get into the runoff.

It was thought that Jimmy Carter, being a moderate, would have a good chance of winning a runoff against either the liberal Ellis Arnall or the conservative Lester Maddox. Carter had finished the campaign strong. It was just a question of whether he had finished strong enough to make it into the runoff.

I had just started my junior year at Fort Valley High School. My Momma and Daddy had agreed to let me fly from Macon to Atlanta on Election Day, so that I could be at Carter headquarters on election night and then fly back to the Macon airport around midnight.

Needless to say, I was very excited. I remember how surprised I was when I got off the elevator at the headquarters floor and saw that Jeff had put up a big poster he had made that said, "Welcome Back, Dugan!" He had put some balloons around it, too. It was very nice of him, and it still means lot to me.

The atmosphere was festive and everybody was in a good mood. This wasn't because we were confident that Jimmy Carter would make it into the runoff.

We were celebrating the fact that we had all done the very best we could. Jimmy Carter had come a long way from the beginning of the summer when some members of The Atlanta Press Club could not even understand him very well.

Now, Jimmy Carter was known and liked by voters all over Georgia. He had earned the opportunity to play a big role in Georgia's future, and we all knew he would take full advantage of it. However, none of us would have believed that in just ten years Jimmy Carter would be elected President of the United States.

As the vote counting began, we got excited about something else. Carter was doing much better than anybody expected. It looked like he might get into the runoff with Arnall.

The night went by very quickly. Soon, it was time for me to tell everybody good bye. After that, I remember walking down the hall with Jeff before leaving for the airport.

When I got on the Delta plane for the short flight to Macon, I was very excited about Carter's chances of making it into the runoff. However, halfway to Macon, I heard a loud explosion on the plane that took my mind completely off of politics.

It sounded like a bomb had gone off on the plane. I was sitting on the back row. My short life flashed in front of my eyes. Then the stewardess came and sat down beside me, fastened her seat belt very tightly, and started smoking. I thought that was a bad sign.

The pilot announced that the plane was turning around and going back to the Atlanta airport. When we landed in Atlanta, we were told that the back door of the propeller-driven plane had not been closed properly and had blown off.

The airline told us to wait in the passenger area, while another plane was brought to fly us to Macon. Not many of the passengers opted to take the second flight, so I had my choice of seats. I sat on the front row, even though I don't know what good I thought that could do if the plane crashed.

When we landed in Macon, I met my Daddy. He told me that the final votes had come in and that it was Maddox, not Carter, who would be in the runoff with Arnall. I was disappointed, but still proud of the great job Carter had done in the campaign.

Georgia had open primaries, which meant that any registered voter could vote in the Democratic Party runoff. Many Republicans, who had voted for Bo Callaway in the Republican primary, crossed over and voted for Maddox in the Democratic runoff.

The Republicans thought their party's nominee, Bo Callaway, would have a better chance of beating Maddox in the general election in November than he would have of beating Arnall.

As a result, Maddox upset Arnall in the runoff to win the Democratic Party's nomination for Governor. However, many people believed that it was cross-over Republicans and not Democrats who had given the Democratic nomination to Maddox.

The Democratic progressives and liberals were so furious about this that they organized a write-in campaign for Ellis Arnall in the general election. In the general election, Callaway came in first with 46.5% of the vote, Maddox came in second with 46.2%, and Arnall received 7%.

Under Georgia law, a majority vote in the general election was required for a candidate to be elected Governor. Since nobody won a majority, the law provided that the state legislature had to meet and choose between the two top finishers, Republican Callaway and Democrat Maddox, in what was called a contingent election.

This was high political drama, and it caught the attention of the national media. On January 9, 1967, Miss Rosalynn wrote me a letter from Plains, which I am looking at as I write this.

After going over a few personal items, she wrote me that Jimmy Carter was in Atlanta, because he had been asked to help with the telecasting of the election by the legislature the next day. She said she thought he would enjoy it.

She also wrote that it looked like Maddox would be the next Governor. She added that we would have to reconcile ourselves to this fact, but could take satisfaction from the fact that we had tried to save our state from the situation.

The vast majority of the members of the Georgia legislature were Democrats. So, just as Miss Rosalynn had predicted in her letter to me, they stayed loyal to the Democratic Party and elected

Lester Maddox Governor of Georgia by a vote of 182 to 66.

That day finished the 1966 campaign for Governor. But, it also kicked off the 1970 campaign for the same high office, because Jimmy Carter never stopped running.

# Chapter 12

## Man and Politician

The purpose of this book is to help people appreciate Jimmy Carter the way I did. I think the thoughts in this chapter might be helpful in that regard.

Of course, you need to understand that there were many people who were much closer to Jimmy Carter than I was. They may have memories that are different from mine. I'm only speaking for myself.

I don't remember Jimmy Carter ever laughing really hard. I don't remember him ever saying anything really funny.

In speeches, he would sometimes try to be witty. Often the audience laughed politely, but I never saw him break up a crowd. It was not his gift.

I don't think I ever heard him use the word love except in speeches. Love was a something he expressed through his actions, not his words.

Jimmy Carter was never a great speaker in the conventional sense. He did not use emotion to rouse a crowd. But, his speeches were very high on substance. He always had an amazing command of the details involved in the subject about which he was speaking. In his speeches, he talked just like he did in a one-on-one meeting.

Jimmy Carter kept his cards close to his vest. You had to really examine what he was doing to understand what he was thinking.

I never saw Jimmy Carter get mad. But, I did see him when he was frustrated with me in the 1970 campaign.

He had sent me from Atlanta to pick something up and bring it to him in Plains. The place I had to pick this item up was in such a remote part of the mountains of north Georgia that the only way to get there from Atlanta was to go through Chattanooga, Tennessee.

After I picked the item up, I had to drive back through Chattanooga and then down to Plains. I got there in the middle of the night.

Jimmy Carter was waiting for me outside on his porch. He could not understand why I was so late in getting to Plains.

I told him that I had driven the speed limit the whole way. He looked at me in a way that gave me the distinct impression that he thought my arriving at his home on time was more important than following the speed limit.

He worked very hard and demanded results from himself. He expected the same from the people who worked for him.

Jimmy Carter was driven to make a difference in the world. I think this came primarily from his religious beliefs. But, I think he also had a desire to break down the stereotypical image most people had of Southerners.

Jimmy Carter used his love for the South as a motivation to be the very best person he could be, so that people all over the world could no longer stereotype Southerners based on the demagoguery of many of the South's other politicians. He wanted to give the people of the world a Southern politician they could respect and admire. He accomplished that goal.

When Jimmy Carter gave his inaugural address after being sworn in as Governor of Georgia in 1971, he declared, "I say to you quite frankly that the time for racial discrimination is over." This was the beginning of his effort to show the world that Southern politicians should no longer be stereotyped because of the way many of them had acted in the past.

Jimmy Carter's professions before politics had been submariner and farmer. Those jobs demand planning and execution, not eloquence or sentimentality.

They were also good jobs for loners. I always thought that Jimmy Carter was a loner and an outsider. He was an outsider when he was Governor and when he was President. Outwardly, he appeared to be more analytical than emotional. Of course, in his heart, he was very emotional.

Jimmy Carter was a very wise man with very good judgment. He knew his opportunity to change things related to matters like civil rights would come only after he had the power of being Governor, not while he was trying to acquire that office.

His approach proved to be very effective in healing the wounds that had divided our people for far too long. He also united the sections of our country in a way that no other politician ever had.

# CHAPTER 13

## A Visit to Plains

After the primary campaign ended on September 13, 1966, I continued to have contact with Jimmy Carter and his family. I don't remember many of these visits, but I have some letters from Jimmy Carter, Miss Rosalynn and Jeff that I have kept all these years that remind me of my ongoing relationship with them.

On October 5, 1966, Jimmy Carter wrote me a very nice letter. He said that he didn't think he had adequately thanked me for helping him in his campaign.

In that letter, Jimmy Carter also wrote me of his "bitter disappointment of losing the Governor's race." He was a most competitive man, and he detested losing so much that it caused him real pain.

I think that right after the election he was exhausted and was happy that he had done so much better than people expected him to do. But, after he got a few weeks of rest, he started thinking about how close he had come to getting into the runoff and going on to being elected Governor in 1966.

I think Jimmy Carter equated losing with failing. Fortunately, instead of being bitter, he was able to use that feeling to push himself even harder than he had before to achieve his goals.

Jimmy Carter did the same thing right after he lost his Presidential re-election campaign to Ronald Reagan. Only after that defeat, he had to change the goal that he would push himself to achieve.

I told Jimmy Carter one time that, after he lost the 1980 election, I had prayed and asked God why He would allow such a great Christian man to lose a job in which he could do so much good. I told then former President Carter that the answer I got to that prayer was that God had something even more important than being President that He wanted Carter to do. I think that the passing years proved that was the truth.

Jimmy Carter had dictated and signed that letter, but Miss Rosalynn had typed it and addressed the envelope by hand. They were two very ambitious people committed as one to achieve success.

On November 22, 1966, Jeff wrote me a letter.

He touched on my favorite team, The Georgia Tech Yellow Jackets. Jeff also liked Tech, because Jimmy Carter had gone to Tech before he went to the Naval Academy.

In fact, when Jimmy Carter was President, he went to a football game between Georgia Tech and Navy. He sat on the Tech side in the first half and on the Navy side in the second half.

Jeff said he had just finished a book report on President U.S. Grant. He didn't show any sign that his family's new found notoriety had gone to his head.

On March 6, 1967, Jeff wrote me another letter saying that Jimmy Carter had just left for Fort Valley. He said he wanted to come along, but that his dad had left before he got out of school.

That letter was written on the stationary of Carter's Warehouse. It listed the business as offering "Certified Seed Peanuts, Custom Peanut Shelling, Peanut Buying and Storage, Liquid Nitrogen, Bulk Fertilizer and Lime, Corn Buying, Custom Grinding and Mixing, Cotton Ginning, and Fire and Casualty Insurance." That was Jimmy Carter's family business.

Jeff wrote me that his school situation was "AMUTTOP," which he said meant "abnormally messed up thanks to our principal."

He also said that he had walked to a tennis court and played tennis the night before. He said that was the most exciting thing that had happened in Plains since the campaign.

He wrote that I wouldn't like Plains because "nothing ever happens here." He underlined "ever" two times. He also said that his parents had bought a new car just the week before and had already put over one thousand miles on it.

We had no idea that in ten years Jeff wouldn't be able to go out by himself so easily at night and that Plains would have become one of the busiest places in America. This place where Jeff wrote me that nothing ever happened would soon be full of nationally known TV reporters, visiting political figures, and lots of tourists.

I think this letter shows that Jimmy and Rosalynn Carter were good parents and that Jeff was a well adjusted young man. It didn't seem to me that the Carters had let Jimmy Carter's new found fame change them very much. If anything, it just meant more work for them all and less time together.

The next contact I remember having with Jimmy Carter was the following letter he wrote to me.

August 15, 1967

Dear Steve:

We have been reminiscing lately about the campaign last year and all of us feel that your involvement was an inspiration to our entire campaign organization. I mention you often in my speeches throughout the state as an example of outstanding young Georgians and their potential effectiveness in politics and government.

I am already campaigning in a quiet way and I depend on your future support in all my plans. I need for you to write me frequently and to give me the benefit of your advice and opinions as an expression from young Georgians.

All of us would like for you to visit our home for a week-end whenever you can come.

Sincerely,

Jimmy

JC/rc

This letter was written only eight months after the end of Jimmy Carter's 1966 campaign and over three years before the next election for Governor in 1970. But, it left no doubt that Jimmy Carter was already running for Governor again.

After I got this letter, I started visiting the Carters in Plains. I remember one visit in particular. It was in early 1968. I don't know why I remember this visit so well, but I do.

Very early that Saturday morning, Jimmy Carter and I were sitting alone in his very modest office at the back of the Carter's Warehouse store on the main street in Plains. He was wearing khaki pants, a red flannel shirt, and boots. It was very cold in his office, and he had a wood burning stove in the corner of that little room.

He was sitting behind an old wooden desk. I was sitting across from him. On the wall behind him, he had put up a large map of Georgia that showed all 159 counties in the state.

He had colored each county a certain color based on what percentage of the vote he had received in that county in the 1966 primary election. He explained to me that the map helped him decide in which counties he needed to campaign the most.

Jimmy Carter told me he was already driving all around the state to make speeches two or three nights a week. That had to be exhausting and it had to consume much of Carter's energy and time.

In land area, Georgia is the biggest state east of the Mississippi River. But, that did not keep Jimmy Carter from crisscrossing it day after day and night after night. He was on a mission.

I don't remember any small talk or joking that day. It was all business. Jimmy Carter was talking about his political strategy. I don't even remember saying anything, even though I must have.

While we were talking, Jimmy Carter's oldest son, Jack, knocked on Carter's office door. When he came in, he was dressed in what looked to me like a white Navy uniform and was carrying a big white cloth sack which seemed full of clothes. I think he was also wearing a white cap.

He said, "Well, Dad, I'm leaving for the Great Lakes." Jimmy Carter stood up, smiled at his oldest son, and said a few words. Then, Jack left, and Carter went back to talking about political strategy with me.

I'm sure that when a husband and father is a submariner, his family has to get used to farewells. But, it struck me as very different from the emotional farewells I had experienced with my Momma and Daddy growing up in my family.

I would not have been willing to sacrifice so much time with my family in order to become Governor or President or to win the Nobel Prize. I learned to never envy famous people, because they and the members of their families pay a gigantic price to get where they are.

After we finished talking in his office, Jimmy Carter took me on a walk on some of his land outside of Plains. The only person we saw on our long walk was Dan Reeves.

Reeves had played football at Americus High School near Plains, played quarterback for the South Carolina Gamecocks, and played eight years for the Dallas Cowboys. He would soon become the head coach of the Denver Broncos.

Jimmy Carter introduced me to Dan Reeves. We all talked for a few minutes. Then, Reeves walked in one direction and resumed hunting, and Carter and I kept walking in the other direction and continued to talk about politics.

Jimmy Carter told me that he had given Reeves special permission to hunt on his land. Carter loved his land. I think he felt more comfortable walking in his fields than he did doing anything else.

As with many farmers across America, three things were exceptionally important to Jimmy Carter. They were his faith, his family, and his land.

This gave Jimmy Carter something in common with many people he met on the campaign trail. He was completely sincere about these things, and the farmers he met could tell he was one of them.

This didn't just win him supporters in Georgia. It also gave him a surprise victory in the Iowa caucuses when he ran for the Democratic Party's presidential nomination in 1976.

# CHAPTER 14

## The Convention

In 1968, Governor Lester Maddox of Georgia had a problem. As a Democratic Governor, he had the responsibility to appoint people to be delegates to The Democratic National Convention in Chicago.

However, he was expected to support the third party candidacy of Alabama Governor George Wallace in the Presidential election that year. Therefore, any delegation he selected would face high scrutiny and opposition at the convention.

To try to assemble a diverse delegation more acceptable to the national Democratic Party, Maddox asked Jimmy Carter to suggest some people he could appoint as delegates. Carter suggested that

Maddox appoint me and his cousin, State Senator Hugh Carter of Plains.

Hugh Carter had an antique store right beside Carter's Warehouse on the main street in Plains. When Jimmy Carter became President, Hugh Carter's son worked for Jimmy Carter in The White House.

My Daddy was at a conference in Atlanta when the program was suddenly interrupted. The moderator announced that Daddy had an important phone call from the Governor.

When Daddy picked up the phone, Governor Lester Maddox asked if Daddy would allow him to appoint me as a full voting delegate to the convention in Chicago. He promised Daddy that he would keep me safe by keeping me with him wherever he went.

Daddy agreed, and it was announced that the Governor had appointed me as a delegate. I was 17 at that time, but would be 18 when the convention started.

The person most annoyed with this was our mailman. Within a few days of being appointed, I started getting over 100 letters and packages a day.

My mother and I would open them when I got home from school every day. I got many books inscribed to me by the candidates, including Vice President Hubert Humphrey and a number of others such as Senators Edmund Muskie, Eugene McCarthy and George McGovern.

The mail that we enjoyed opening the most were the letters and packages addressed to "Mrs. Steve Dugan." These invited my non-existent wife to all sorts of interesting events in Chicago while I would be occupied by the convention.

When it came time to leave for Chicago, all the Georgia delegates met in a special room in the Atlanta airport. Then we got on our charter flight.

Before we landed in Chicago, the pilot announced that we were landing at a military airfield because of all the dangerous rioting going on in Chicago. We were told that when we got off the plane we should run through a corridor formed by two columns of armed soldiers until we got safely inside the airport terminal.

As I was running from the plane between the two lines of armed soldiers towards the terminal, I passed a jazz band. The members of this band were wearing red vests and straw hats and playing a rousing version of "Chicago." It was a bizarre situation.

We all made it into the terminal. Then we were placed on military busses and escorted by police cars to our hotel in the middle of Chicago. The hotel was surrounded by rioters and soldiers.

Governor Maddox was determined to keep me close to him as he had promised my Daddy that he would do to keep me safe. So, I found myself staying in his hotel suite.

Governor Maddox had declared that he was a candidate for the Democratic nomination for President. So, he told me to come with him while he went to other hotels and tried to address some of the other states' delegations.

The Secret Service then informed Governor Maddox that there were many serious threats on his life. Because of this danger, they suggested that he not visit the other states' delegations in their hotels.

However, Governor Maddox would not change his mind. The Secret Service agents then said they would get us out of our hotel and into a specially armored Secret Service car as quickly as possible.

I still remember getting to the door of our hotel. I could see the big Secret Service car we were supposed to get into and all the rioters and police surrounding it.

The Secret Service agents with us inside the front door of our hotel were talking with the agents in the car. All of a sudden, they yelled "Go! Go! Go!"

The next thing I knew I was being literally pushed through the air head first into the backseat of the Secret Service car, while the agents kept yelling "Down! Down! Keep your head down!" Governor Maddox had kept his word to Daddy by keeping me right next to him. But, since people were trying to assassinate him, it might not have been the scenario my Daddy had envisioned.

After calling on a handful of state delegations, many of which voted not to let Governor Maddox even speak to them, we were escorted back to Governor Maddox's suite in our hotel. The minute we were safely ensconced in Governor Maddox's suite, he called Governor George Wallace of Alabama to fill him in on what was happening.

Governor Wallace told Governor Maddox that he was doing a great job by showing up at these state delegations and being told that he would not be allowed to speak. Wallace said he thought that would cause a lot of traditional conservative Democrats to vote for him instead of the Democratic candidate in November.

When it came time for our delegation to go to the convention, we got on special busses and headed to the International Amphitheatre. It was surrounded by barbed wire, 11,000 Chicago police officers, and 6,000 armed men from the Illinois National Guard.

When we finally made it to the convention floor, I was amazed by how small it was. I was able to walk around and talk to many famous politicians and celebrities who were delegates from different states. Since I had a delegate badge just like theirs, they were all willing to talk with me.

Paul Newman took a close look at me and asked, "How old are you, Mr. Dugan?"

When I got on the bus waiting to take us back to our hotel, I was sitting beside Hugh Carter of Plains. A first cousin of Jimmy Carter, he had succeeded Jimmy Carter in the State Senate in 1967.

We were ready to go home. On the way back, we talked about Jimmy Carter's campaign to be elected Governor in 1970.

We were sad that it appeared that this convention had hurt the ties between the national Democratic Party and the Georgia Democratic Party. But, we need not have been concerned.

At the very next Democratic Convention just four years later in Miami, then-Governor Jimmy Carter of Georgia would rehabilitate Georgia's reputation in the national Democratic Party.

He was asked to nominate Washington Senator Henry M. "Scoop" Jackson for President. Jimmy Carter did so, even though another Southerner, Alabama Governor George Wallace, was also a candidate for President at that convention.

When Senator George McGovern won the nomination, Jimmy Carter received convention votes to be the party's nominee for Vice President. It was at that convention that Jimmy Carter began to be seen as a national Democrat. Unlike many other

Southern politicians, Jimmy Carter was emerging from the restrictive label of being just a regional leader.

Then, four years after that and eight years after Hugh Carter and I were delegates to the raucous 1968 Democratic Convention in Chicago, the national Democratic Party nominated Jimmy Carter for President of The United States on the first ballot of a unified and harmonious convention.

Of course, if someone had told Hugh Carter and me while we were on that bus leaving the 1968 Democratic Convention that in eight years the Democratic Party would nominate Jimmy Carter for President, we would not have believed it. It wouldn't have seemed possible.

# CHAPTER 15

## A Real Friend

On July 7, 1969, Jimmy Carter wrote me another letter, which I still have. In it, he invited me to a meeting to discuss his campaign plans for the 1970 election for Governor.

I'm sure I went to the meeting, but I don't have any memory of it. The next contact I remember with Jimmy Carter was when he invited me to visit him and his family in Plains the weekend before Christmas in 1969.

When I got to the Carter's home that Saturday morning and walked towards their door, I noticed some bright lights shining through their living room windows. When I walked in, I saw Jimmy

Carter sitting in his easy chair holding his two year old daughter, Amy, in his lap.

The bright lights I had seen came from a film crew getting footage of Jimmy Carter at home with his family. That film was used in making TV commercials for the coming campaign. Unlike Carter's 1966 campaign, his 1970 campaign was a very professional operation.

I contrasted this in my mind with the 1966 campaign. That year, Carter didn't even decide to run for Governor until March, and he didn't have the money to make professional commercials like the ones I saw being made in his home that Saturday before Christmas in 1969.

While he was filming commercials, I watched Nebraska beat the Georgia Bulldogs 45 to 6 in The Sun Bowl. Being a Georgia Tech fan, I took the final score a lot better than some of the other people in the house.

When Jimmy Carter finished filming commercials, Carter and I talked about how the campaign was shaping up. This was a different situation entirely from the 1966 race.

In the 1966 campaign, Jimmy Carter made a name for himself throughout Georgia by doing much better than anybody had thought he could. But in 1970, the pressure was on Carter to win.

If he lost, he might not get another chance. There couldn't be another morale victory in 1970. He had to win.

On the positive side, Jimmy Carter had a much more well financed and organized campaign for the looming 1970 race. He had also been going all over Georgia making speeches and meeting people in preparation for his 1970 campaign since early in 1967.

On the negative side, however, Jimmy Carter was going up against a very strong and well financed opponent, former Governor Carl Sanders. Sanders had been Governor from 1963 through 1966.

The only thing that kept Sanders from running for Governor in 1966 was Georgia's legal prohibition against governors running for consecutive terms. Because of this, Sanders had to sit out the 1966 election. However, he was the big favorite to win in 1970.

Throughout Jimmy Carter's political career, he has always been the underdog, and his opponents have always underestimated him. His weaknesses such as not being a rousing speaker were highly visible.

However, Jimmy Carter had some strengths that were harder to recognize, such as his unrivaled work ethic. It had driven him to make all those hundreds of mostly unpublicized trips to meet people all over Georgia in the preceding three years.

Jimmy Carter's unusually strong impact on people when he met them on-on-one was another very important campaign strength that flew under his opponents' radar. When he had a conversation with a voter, he let the voter do most of the talking, and Carter did most of the listening. People liked that. They sensed he was being himself and not putting on an act.

During that Christmas week visit to Jimmy Carter in Plains, I became convinced that Carter was confident that he would upset Carl Sanders in the Democratic Primary in 1970 and then win the general election. But, I knew that Carl Sanders was confident that he would win, too.

During our talks that weekend, Jimmy Carter asked me to work for him full time out of his Atlanta headquarters during the coming summer and fall. I told him that I really wanted to, but that I needed to earn some money while doing so.

He understood. We agreed that I would report to his Atlanta headquarters as soon as I finished my sophomore year of college in Virginia that spring.

Jimmy Carter told me that my friend, Hamilton Jordan, was going to be his campaign manager. Carter also said the campaign might use me to go around the state and make speeches at events to which he was invited but could not attend because of other commitments he had to attend bigger events. I was looking forward to the job and also looking forward to spending more time with Hamilton.

I think I might have spent that Saturday night at Miss Lillian's house out in the country. After talking with Jimmy Carter some more the next day, I drove back home to Fort Valley.

What I didn't tell Jimmy Carter during that visit was that I had something a lot more important on my mind than politics during those days. I had fallen in love with a girl named Julie Cole. The problem was that Julie was not in love with me.

During the early spring of 1970, I went to spend a weekend with Julie and her parents at their house in Newnan, Georgia. I had never spent a weekend at a girl's house before, so I hoped Julie was beginning to love me.

On that Sunday, she walked me down to her parents' garage, where I was going to get in my car and drive back to Lexington, Virginia. I was attending Washington and Lee University.

When we said good bye, Julie told me that she was never going to love me. She said that she thought she was falling in love with somebody else.

I was devastated. I am an emotional person. I cried all the way from Newnan to Charlotte, North Carolina, which I considered to be the half-way point of the trip.

When I stopped to get gasoline in Charlotte, I called Jimmy Carter at his house in Plains. I told him the whole story.

I told Jimmy Carter that I wanted to leave Washington and Lee and return to Georgia right away. He listened to everything I had to say and was very patient.

Then, Jimmy Carter said, "Why don't you just leave Washington and Lee and come to Plains and live with us? You can start working on the campaign right now."

Jimmy Carter told me that my friend Hamilton Jordan was already working on the campaign. I told

Carter that I would quit Washington and Lee and be at his house later that week to start working for him.

The next day, I called my parents and told them the news. They were very upset with my decision. They wanted me to stay at Washington and Lee.

So, I called Jimmy Carter and told him that I would not be coming to Plains and moving into his house after all. I told Carter I would report to his headquarters in Atlanta and begin working full time for his campaign as soon as the school year ended.

The Carters had a nice house in Plains, but it was not a mansion. They had a lot to do and a big family.

Yet, when I needed him, Jimmy Carter did not hesitate for a second to offer to let me move into his home and start working for his campaign as soon as I could get there. He didn't check with Miss Rosalynn or ask for time to think about it.

When I called Jimmy Carter out of the blue on that Sunday night, I had just wanted to talk with a friend. It had not even occurred to me that it was even possible that Jimmy Carter would instantly come up with a solution to my problem, especially one that would involve what I considered a big sacrifice for both him and his family.

However, that was one of the secrets of Jimmy Carter's success. There was almost no priority on earth more important to him than a friend who needed help.

Jimmy Carter did not show his emotions with words, which is what I always did. He held himself to a much higher standard of friendship than I did.

Jimmy Carter was a man of quick analytical thought and decisive action. I don't think I ever saw him hesitate about anything.

He would make a decision instantly and then do whatever he needed to do to follow through on it, no matter how big of a personal sacrifice it required from him. When he helped me, he always seemed like he was the person benefitting the most from what he was doing, not me.

Jimmy Carter helped me this same way many times throughout my life, and he never let me feel like I was a burden to him. There were just three other people who ever treated me in such an unreasonably kind way, and they were my wife and my parents.

Yes, that wonderful girl who said that she could never love me changed her mind. Now, thanks to God, we have been married for over 53 years.

I have often wondered what it would have been like if I had left Washington and Lee and moved in with the Carters that spring. I know I would have learned a lot of lessons and experienced a lot of interesting things. I would have especially enjoyed spending more time with Jeff.

I don't know why Jimmy Carter was always so kind to me. I can't think of anything I had to offer him that he could not have received from anybody else. But, I do know that a friend like Jimmy Carter is a rare gift from God.

# CHAPTER 16

## Speaking For Jimmy Carter

During the 1970 campaign, I spent a lot of my time out on the road, visiting people and making talks about Jimmy Carter.

In the middle of June, I was asked if I would like to start substituting for Jimmy Carter at some speaking engagements to which Carter was invited but could not attend due to a conflict in his schedule.

I was told to write a speech I would like to give. After I did, it was approved by Hamilton Jordan, the campaign manager.

Then, it had to be approved by another man who Jimmy Carter relied on very heavily for advice. He was a very highly respected Atlanta attorney named Charles Kirbo.

I was told to go to Mr. Kirbo's office in downtown Atlanta, answer any questions he might have, and give him a copy of my speech.

I went to Mr. Kirbo's law firm on a sunny summer afternoon. But, when I walked into Mr. Kirbo's office, it was almost dark. The only light in the room was from one small lamp on his desk. He had even muted the light from it by using a very dark green lampshade.

Mr. Kirbo asked me for a copy of my speech. I handed it to him.

When I got back to Jimmy Carter's headquarters, I was told that Mr. Kirbo had approved the speech. I was told that I would be flown to make the speech to a civic group in south Georgia that night.

Before I left for the airport, I was given a prop to use during the speech. It was a "Sanders for Governor" campaign button.

I was shown how to pop off the outer layer of the button that had Carl Sanders' picture on it. After you did that, you could see that it had been superimposed on an old Humphrey for president button left over from the 1968 Presidential campaign.

It turned out that Humphrey had given Sanders thousands of buttons left over from Humphrey's presidential campaign two years before. It saved the Sanders campaign some money to superimpose Sanders' message and likeness on these old Humphrey buttons, rather than to have to make the Sanders buttons from scratch.

However, the buttons made one of the major points of Carter's 1970 campaign. Carter's advisors believed that Sanders was vulnerable because he was associated too closely with the establishment of the national Democratic Party. The average voters in Georgia thought of themselves as Georgia Democrats, not national Democrats.

The majority of voters in Georgia had a lot more in common with a peanut farmer from Plains than they did with a smooth talking big city lawyer.

I enjoyed making that speech all across Georgia. I would always finish it by saying, "In the words of the late, great Tex Ritter, 'God knows the trouble that we're in. God bless America again.'" That always got a standing ovation.

I later found out that Tex Ritter was not dead. But, he had recorded a patriotic song called "God Bless America Again."

Jimmy Carter had shown confidence in me by sending me out to speak for him. I really enjoyed it. I told Hamilton Jordan that when I stood up in front of those crowds, I could feel what the people were thinking. I just said it back to them. Every time

I got ready to leave the headquarters to make a talk, Hamilton would say, "OK, Dugan. Go tell 'um what they think!"

I still take it as a huge compliment that Jimmy Carter trusted me enough to let me speak on his behalf. Public speaking is one of the few things that I can do well and enjoy doing. I liked to say things that people liked to hear.

I knew the crowds that I spoke to were disappointed when they saw me instead of Jimmy Carter get up to speak to them. So, I tried very hard both to entertain them with some good laughs and represent Jimmy Carter well.

I remember getting into a little two seat one propeller airplane that the campaign had arranged to fly me to south Georgia to make a speech for Jimmy Carter. As we took off, I looked down at the city of Atlanta. Then, the pilot turned on the radio.

Legendary Atlanta newsman Aubrey Morris was broadcasting the five o'clock news on WSB radio.

I couldn't believe it when Mr. Morris announced that Jimmy Carter was sending me out on the road to speak for him. I still remember the feeling that gave me. I felt like I was on top of the world, and I knew that I owed it all to the fact that Jimmy Carter trusted me. I did not want to let him down.

# CHAPTER 17

## Other Memories of the 1970 Campaign

Even though I was on the road for a lot of the 1970 campaign, I did have some occasions to do things with Jimmy Carter. For instance, he asked me to ride with him on a float in the July 4th "Salute 2 America" parade in Atlanta sponsored by WSB TV.

I also remember another incident that happened early in the summer. Jimmy Carter was lagging in the polls, and he needed to do something to get some attention for his campaign.

He asked me to go with him to the state capitol for a news conference and to carry his brief case. At the news conference, Jimmy Carter picked up the brief case and put it on the table behind which he was standing.

"In this brief case," Jimmy Carter solemnly told the assembled reporters, "I have clear evidence that Carl Sanders is out of touch with the voters of Georgia."

The reporters asked what was in the brief case. "No," Carter said, "I'm not going to tell you today. I will do that later. I just wanted to let you know I have it."

That was the entire press conference. At that point, Carter left and I followed him. I never heard Carter say anything else about that brief case or what was inside it.

But, Jimmy Carter and his mysterious brief case led off the evening news broadcasts that night. For a campaign that needed some attention, Carter's ploy had worked.

Another thing I remember was being sent on a Saturday afternoon to pick something up from the pastor of a church in south Georgia. I was told to drive around the church three times and blow my horn.

It sounded sort of ridiculous. But, when I drove around the church the third time and blew my horn, the preacher came out the back door of the church.

He was carrying a big box. I opened my trunk, and he put the box inside. Then, he went back into the church, and I drove back to the headquarters in Atlanta.

That summer Hamilton Jordan and I were roommates again. But, this time Jimmy Carter worked it out for us to stay in the home of his Aunt Sissy in the Atlanta suburb of Roswell. Like all the members of the Carter family that I ever met, she was very nice to me.

Jody Powell and Chip Tate had joined the Jimmy Carter campaign. They were smart and fun to spend time with.

Jody Powell had been a student at Emory in 1968, when he sent Jimmy Carter a copy of a paper on Southern populism that he had written. Carter was so impressed that he offered Jody the job of being his volunteer driver.

While driving Jimmy Carter around the state, Jody became good friends with Carter. This led to Jody eventually becoming Carter's press secretary when Carter was Governor, when he ran for President, and when he was in The White House.

Chip Tate had graduated from the University of Virginia law school. My wife, Julie, and I had gotten engaged in early June. The next week, she left on a long-planned three week trip to Japan and other places in the Far East that was led by the President of LaGrange College, where she was a student.

While she was gone, Chip Tate and I went to a lot of movies. I remember us going to see "Patton,"

"Darling Lili," and "Chisum." We also went to some Braves games. I used to walk from the campaign headquarters downtown to Atlanta Stadium to those games.

In spite of all the hard work he had done, Jimmy Carter was considered a big underdog in the 1970 election. The feeling was that former Governor Carl Sanders would win pretty easily.

However, my impression from driving around the state was that Sanders was over confident and out of touch with the average Georgia voters. I remember driving around south Georgia and seeing his supporters' cars with bumper stickers in several pastel colors that said "Sanders Again!"

I thought those bumper stickers seemed more suited for a coronation than for a tough political campaign. I thought they would turn off regular people struggling with problems. That proved to be the case on the night of the Democratic Party primary election.

That night, Jimmy Carter shocked everybody by getting 48% of the votes, and Carl Sanders got 37%. In the runoff, Carter got 59% and Sanders got 40%.

In my opinion, Carter won because he was a great one-on-one campaigner. He ran a grueling and uninterrupted campaign for four entire years leading up to the1970 election.

No politician ever outworked Jimmy Carter. He was an intensely focused and driven man. He had good intentions to help people, but he knew he had to win the election to put his plans into action.

Looking back on it, I also believe that God had a great plan for Jimmy Carter's life. Getting elected Governor in 1970 was a necessary part of it.

# Chapter 18

## A Big Regret

I was having a great time in the campaign, but I had something else that was even more important to me going on in my life. Early that June, Julie and I had gotten engaged. Late in the summer, we decided to get married on September 19.

In the middle of August, Hamilton Jordan told me that the campaign was almost broke. He asked me if I would keep working without pay until the primary election, which would be in September.

I told Hamilton that I had to make some money, because I was going to need it when I got married just five weeks later. Therefore, I said that I had no choice but to try to find another job for the rest of the summer.

I can't even tell you how ashamed I feel about that decision. Yes, I needed to make some money. But, every single time I ever asked Jimmy Carter to help me, Carter always went out of his way to do everything he could for me.

Now, when he needed my help, I said "no." If I could see him one more time, I would apologize for this. It makes me feel so bad just to think about it.

However, it just created one more situation in which Jimmy Carter showed me what a great person he was. He and Miss Rosalynn gave Julie and me a beautiful silver serving tray for a wedding present.

Jimmy Carter never held this against me. As you will see, he continued to be my friend and to help me every time I needed help throughout my life. But, it makes me feel disloyal that I didn't stick with the campaign when he asked me to do so.

Leaving the campaign was one of the worst and most selfish decisions I ever made in my life. Fortunately, it was not the end of my friendship with Jimmy Carter. But, it was the last time I was on Jimmy Carter's staff.

When Jimmy Carter was sworn in as Governor in January of 1971, I was in the middle of my junior year at The University of Georgia in Athens. Julie and I had just been married for a few months, and I was very happy. But, since I had not finished college, I wouldn't have been able to go to work for Governor Jimmy Carter at that time, even if he had asked me to do so.

I have often wondered what might have happened if I had not left the campaign. Would Jimmy Carter have offered me a job in his administration? Would I have gotten to work for him from the time he became

Governor until his term as President ended, like Hamilton Jordan and Jody Powell did?

I think Jimmy Carter probably would have given me the chance to do those things. He did offer me a job at the start of his Presidential campaign. But, looking back on my life, there is one big reason that I am not sorry that I did not do those things.

As great as it would have been to work for Jimmy Carter during all those exciting times, it would have caused me to miss spending so much time with Julie. I wouldn't have traded spending that time with Julie for anything, not even for the opportunity to work in The White House.

# CHAPTER 19

## Two Paths

After I finished college, I got drafted. By the time I finished my active duty training, it was the fall of 1973.

At that time, Congressman Jack Brinkley gave me a job in his district office in Warner Robins, Georgia. Julie and I were very happy in Warner Robins.

One weekend in 1974, Julie and I were visiting her parents in Newnan. That Saturday afternoon, I called The Governor's Mansion in Atlanta and asked to speak with Jimmy Carter. The person who took the call told me that Governor and Mrs. Carter were out and would not be back that night.

That night, about 2:30 AM, I heard the phone ring. I heard my Father-In-Law answer it. Then, he knocked on our door and said the phone was for me.

I was worried that somebody in our family had died, or that something else bad had happened. When I picked up the phone, I said, "Hello."

The voice on the phone said, "Hello, Steve. This is Jimmy."

Then Jimmy Carter asked me if Julie and I could meet him at a farm in middle Georgia the next afternoon. I told him we would be there.

When we got there, Jimmy Carter was waiting for us. He was talking with some people about raising money.

I didn't know what he was planning. He couldn't run for reelection as Governor, because the Georgia Constitution prevented Governors from succeeding themselves. The only elective office in Georgia that might appeal to him would be U.S. Senator. But, Georgia had two very popular Senators at that time.

We had a nice visit with Governor Carter that day. But, neither my wife nor I understood exactly why he had wanted to see us. However, I should have gotten a clue from something he said.

Jimmy Carter said he had been inviting prominent national Democrats that came to Atlanta to spend the night at The Governor's Mansion. He said that he would stay up late at night talking with them and then talk with them some more the next morning at breakfast.

These national Democratic leaders may have thought Jimmy Carter was being hospitable. But, that wasn't Carter's main reason for inviting them to stay at The Governor's Mansion.

Jimmy Carter said he used his time with these prominent Democrats at The Governor's Mansion to size them up. He said he did not feel intimidated by any of them.

Some time after this meeting, I got a call from Hamilton Jordan. He asked me to meet him at a large warehouse outside of Atlanta.

I told him that I would meet him, but I had no idea what he had in mind. At that time nobody but a very few people knew what Jimmy Carter was planning. When I got there, Hamilton met me.

There was nobody else around this huge warehouse. Hamilton unlocked the door. When he turned on the lights, I could see that this large building was filled with Carter for President signs and other things that would be needed in a presidential campaign.

Hamilton told me that Jimmy Carter was going to run for President. He told me that Carter wanted me to work in his campaign. He offered me a job.

I looked at Hamilton and laughed. I said, "Look, Hamilton. I'm married now. I've got a job. I can't do crazy stuff like this anymore. You're going to have a great time for three months. Then, you'll run out of money and that will be the end of the campaign. I can't turn my life upside down for that."

I had no idea of the incredible amount of preparation that Jimmy Carter, Hamilton Jordan and a few other people had put into this Presidential campaign.

On August 4, 1974, Hamilton had written a brilliant and detailed 112 page memo to Jimmy Carter in which he went over everything that related to Carter's upcoming Presidential campaign. It exhausted me just to read it.

Clearly, Jimmy Carter and Hamilton Jordan were very serious. I should never have laughed about the subject when Hamilton told me about it.

But, as I said, even knowing what I know now, I am not sorry that I did not join the Carter Presidential campaign. You only get so much time in this life, and spending my time with my wife and soon to be born sons doing ordinary things made me happier than anything else could have.

After this, my relationship with Jimmy Carter was limited to just being a friend. To me, however, the things that Jimmy Carter went far out of his way to do for me as my friend meant more to me than all the things that he could have ever done for me in politics, including giving me a job working at The White House.

# Chapter 20

## Reunion At The White House

After I graduated from law school in 1980, I started working in Washington as a Legislative Assistant for Congressman Jack T. Brinkley of Georgia. Later on in this book, I will describe more about my friendship with him.

On December 12, 1980, I called Hugh Carter in Plains. He was Jimmy Carter's cousin and had become a State Senator. I told him that I was working in Washington for Congressman Brinkley and that I would like to talk with President Carter. Later that afternoon, I got a call from President Carter's secretary telling me that President Carter wanted me to come to The White House to visit with him.

I took a cab from The Rayburn House Office Building beside the Capitol to The White House. I am going to describe what happened when I got to The White House, because it was very exciting to me.

The cab dropped me off at a guard house right beside the entrance to The White House grounds.

The guard asked me for my identification. When I showed it to him, he looked on a list he had.

When he saw that my name was on the list, he told me to just come in the gate. At that point, I was on The White House lawn. But, I was still a short walk away from the entrance to the West Wing, where the Oval Office is located.

There was nobody else on The White House lawn but me. It was an unbelievable feeling. As I walked up the grassy hill towards the plain door to the West Wing, I felt like the prodigal son returning home to his father.

When I got to the door to the West Wing, there was just one Marine guard in a dress uniform guarding it. He opened the door, and I walked in.

The waiting room was surprisingly small and modest. I was the only person sitting there.

President Carter's secretary came and told me that the President would see me in a few minutes. From where I was sitting, I could see into the empty Cabinet Room across the hall. I was surprised at how small and informal these famous rooms were.

As I continued to wait, the door through which I entered opened. It was Vice President Walter Mondale returning from lunch.

A few minutes later, my old friend Hamilton Jordan walked into the waiting room and we talked for a few minutes. Then, President Carter's secretary came and got me and took me into the Oval Office.

Finally, after six years, I was back having a one-on-one visit with Jimmy Carter. It had been fourteen years since we had met for the first time at that Affirmation Vietnam rally at the Fort Valley High School gym.

President Carter had the weight of the world on his shoulders. Trying to get the hostages freed was keeping him from getting much sleep and using up all of his energy.

But, when we looked in each other's eyes, he got a big grin on his face. President Carter could not have been nicer to me than he was that day.

It was just like no time had passed at all. President Carter said that he was about to go to Camp David.

President Carter asked me to walk into the Rose Garden with him, where he was going to board the Presidential helicopter, Marine One. Then he called The White House photographer and asked him to take some pictures of the two of us.

I still have one of those photographs today. When I look at it, I can see a happy look on President Carter's face.

After his helicopter flew away, I walked back into the Oval Office. There was no one else in that famous room but me.

I took my time and looked around carefully, because I did not think that I would ever be back. I could physically feel the presence of all the great Americans who I knew had been in that room before me.

A few days later, I got another call from President Carter's secretary. She said the President wanted me to come back to the White House to get a copy of the photograph that had been taken of the two of us. The White House photographer gave me several copies of the picture that President Carter had selected. He wrote a personal note to me on one of the copies of that photograph. Somehow, I have lost that copy, but I still have the unsigned ones.

I had failed Jimmy Carter when he asked me to work without pay towards the end of his 1970 campaign for Governor of Georgia. I had disappointed him again when he asked me to join his Presidential campaign staff.

Then, I had run for Congress as a Republican during the same campaign year that Jimmy Carter ran for President as a Democrat. Not many people in President Carter's position would have forgiven me for all those things and continued to be my friend.

But, Jimmy Carter never stopped being my friend. As you will see, his greatest acts of friendship to me were in the future.

# CHAPTER 21

## True Friendship

The next time I remember seeing Jimmy Carter was in July of 1988. He and Miss Rosalynn came to Columbus, Georgia for a book signing.

Julie and I took our two sons to meet them. A few days later, Miss Rosalynn wrote us a nice note, which both she and President Carter signed.

I still have this note. I had given both President Carter and Mrs. Carter a copy of a little book I liked called "God's Promises."

Miss Rosalynn wrote, "Thank you so much for the book of God's Promises and for your kind words."

The kind words that Miss Rosalynn referred to were probably just me saying how proud I was of them. I don't remember exactly what I told them, but I know that it was sincere.

I think Jimmy Carter always knew that I was absolutely sincere in everything that I ever told him. I knew that he was absolutely sincere in what he said to me, too.

Maybe it was something as simple as my sincerity that caused him to be so kind to me. I don't know.

What I do know is that Jimmy and Rosalynn Carter believed in going the extra mile where friendship was concerned. It took time from her busy schedule for Miss Rosalynn to write me that note.

It also took time for Jimmy Carter to read it and write "Jimmy" beside Miss Rosalynn's name. For some reason that I will never understand, it was important for both of them to take the time to write and sign that card.

At the time of that visit, our family was riding high. By June of 2001, I had sunk into a deep depression. I never thought about committing suicide, but I did feel like everybody that I loved would be better off if I died.

At that dark hour, a wonderful person that I worked with in Washington for Congressman Brinkley heard about our situation and arranged for me to meet with her father, who was a very wealthy Christian man.

Julie and I went to Columbus to meet with him. He owned a lot of businesses, and I thought that he might give me a job in one of them.

After spending a lot of time talking with us, he saw how bad off I was. He told me that he was willing to get me a job as an assistant janitor at an inner-city outreach program of his church.

He said that he would get Julie a job working in the nursery of the same facility. He said that if we would be willing to do that, he would pay for me to go to an excellent psychologist three times a week and to a very good psychiatrist, too. He also said that he would pay for all of our medicine and medical needs.

He then said that Julie and I should go look at some places we might be able to live, talk about what we wanted to do, and then come back and talk with him again. As down as I was, this was still a difficult pill to swallow.

I had to confront the reality of my situation in a way that I had avoided up until then. It was so hard and painful for me to see how far down I had brought my family. I didn't want to work as an assistant janitor, but I felt like it was the only opportunity I had to try to get my life together again.

Julie was very supportive. She was totally in favor of us following the program this good man had laid out for us. I faced the fact that it was the only option we had to keep our family going but, to be honest, I was not too happy about it.

We were introduced to an elderly and sick man who had a small house. He was very nice to us. He agreed that we could live with him in his house in exchange for us helping to take care of him.

So, Julie, our wonderful golden Labrador, Martina, and I moved into this kind man's house. As soon as we did, Julie and I started working at that community outreach center.

It was a large community center that served underprivileged children. It had a lot of bathrooms and many commodes.

As Assistant Janitor, my job was to clean all the restrooms every day. That's all I did day after day.

At first, I hated it. There was one big bathroom right next to the indoor basketball court that had about six stalls and ten urinals in it.

I hated going into that bathroom to clean it every day. The kids that used it thought the entire room was a bathroom.

One day, as I approached the door to this bathroom pushing my cart of cleaning supplies, I said, "Devil, I hope you have the nastiest bathroom in the history of the world on the other side of this door. I want to show you that there is nothing you can do to keep me from following God's plan for my life."

That was the turning point. After that, I didn't just clean those bathrooms. I attacked them.

I started feeling good about what I was doing. I knew I was doing something of which God approved. That is the greatest feeling in the world.

I liked the people with whom I was working and the children who came there every day, too. When Julie and I got home every afternoon, we had more enjoyment and peace together than we had known in a long time.

Jimmy Carter heard about this. He sent word that he was coming to visit me at this center. He and Mrs. Carter also contributed $1,000 to an effort I had started to help other people like me who had experienced a jolting change in their lives because of mental illness.

My goal was to help those people have a way to receive the same type of encouragement and help to rebuild their lives that I had received. This fit right in with Miss Rosalynn's work to help destigmatize mental illness.

The night that Jimmy Carter arrived with his Secret Service escort, there were many people there to meet him. Someone asked Jimmy Carter if he would make a speech. He said, "I will if Steve Dugan introduces me like he used to."

Well, I tried to introduce Jimmy Carter in the same upbeat way I had years before at all those campaign rallies. But, I got choked up and had to pause several times before I could finish.

I kept thinking about how far I had fallen since the last time I had introduced Jimmy Carter.When I finished, I turned towards Jimmy Carter like I always did after I introduced him.

But, this time there was something extra in Jimmy Carter's eyes. He knew how special his being there was to me, and I think that made him very happy that he had come.

He put his arms around me. The first words he said to the crowd were, "It would have been worth it to me to go anywhere in the world just to be introduced by Steve Dugan one more time."

I am crying as I type these words onto my computer screen. I simply feel so humbled and blessed by God that such a great man as Jimmy Carter would care about me.

Soon, it was time for Jimmy Carter to leave. I walked with him to his Secret Service SUV.

He started to get in. Then he turned around and looked me in the eyes one last time and shook my hand.

That was the last time I ever saw Jimmy Carter. Since there had to be a last time, I'm glad that was it.

Jimmy Carter did not need to take time away from his busy schedule to come to see me at this outreach center. I'm sure there were many more important engagements he had to cancel to come see me. There were no cameras or reporters there. He just went far out of his way to encourage me.

A lot of people have written excellent accounts of the amazing things that Jimmy Carter did in his life. But, this little story is not in any of those books. This story is not about what he did. It is about the kind of person he really was.

I think that when Jimmy Carter gets to Heaven, one of the first things God will say to him is "Thank you for being such a good friend to Steve Dugan. That was Christianity."

# CHAPTER 22

## A Faithful Friend

A few months after Jimmy Carter visited me at that outreach center, the psychologist I was seeing told me that he thought Julie and I should move back to where we lived before and that I should go back to practicing law.

It scared me to think of leaving the relatively pressure-free life we had while we were working at that outreach center. Like I used to tell Julie, "Commodes don't call you when you get home and complain about how you cleaned them."

I prayed about it. I decided that it was time for me to try again to serve God by trying to help people. I also thought it was time for me to try to help Julie and our family by earning some money.

So, Julie, Martina and I loaded up our car and moved to Dauphin Island, Alabama. I started going to the County Courthouse in Mobile every day in the hope that some judges would appoint me to represent indigent defendants in criminal cases.

God touched some of the judges' hearts, and they started appointing me to some cases. I always asked God to be in charge of every case that I got, and I did the very best I could.

Julie was also working at a number of jobs. She cleaned people's houses and took care of their pets when they went out of town.

Together, we were doing pretty well. However, I wanted to get a job with a more predictable income and some health benefits.

I used to go to a men's Bible study group very early in the morning on one day a week. I met some wonderful people there, and they knew that I was trying to find a salaried job with predictable income and health benefits.

Two of these men owned a large lumber company in Mobile. Without telling me anything about what they had in mind, they called a man they knew who was in the lumber business in south Georgia.

They asked him if he knew Jimmy Carter. When he said that he did, they told their friend about my situation and asked him if he would tell former President Carter.

A few days later, one of these men called me and asked me to come to his office. When I got there, he asked me to sit down.

Then, he handed me an envelope. He had a big smile on his face.

I could see that the envelope was from The Carter Center in Atlanta. When I opened it, there was a letter from former President Carter inside.

When I read it, I couldn't believe it. This is what Jimmy Carter had written.

"January 17, 2005

"TO WHOM IT MAY CONCERN:

"Subject Steve Dugan

"I have known Steve Dugan for more than twenty-five years, since he was a student and did a superb job of helping me in my earliest campaign for governor. Subsequently, Steve has gone through law school and is a practicing attorney.

"As much as anyone I have known, Steve has a way of getting to know people, and is an inspiring speaker.

"Steve is deeply religious, and one of the all-too-rare Christians who actually puts his faith into action. He has a remarkable commitment to helping people in need. From the perspective of a highly competitive society, Steve has been overly generous with his time, talent, and financial resources.

"In fact, this strong altruistic inclination has sometimes resulted in Steve's ignoring his own selfinterests.

"I would recommend Steve strongly for any responsible assignment, especially promoting and serving a worthy cause. Although I rarely make such an offer, I would be glad to discuss Steve's characteristics with any prospective employer. I can be reached through my office at The Carter Center in Atlanta, 404-XXX-XXXX.

"Sincerely,

"Jimmy Carter"

I was emotionally overcome by this letter. I thanked my friend for reaching out to President Carter on my behalf.

Then, I went home and showed it to Julie. I said, "I think President Carter has got me confused with somebody else."

I knew myself pretty well. I did believe in God as much as I could, but I was certainly not a very good Christian.

I had not been overly generous with my time, talent and Julie's financial resources, either. To the contrary, I had squandered those things away through sins and horribly foolish decisions.

When I read this letter over several times, I decided that Jimmy Carter was not writing about me as I really was. He knew that I had not been successful and had experienced some major problems. Unfortunately, I just wasn't the person he described in that letter. I wish I had been.

Instead, Jimmy Carter was writing about me as the person I could have been and the person I'm sure that he prayed I might still become. I appreciated that letter very much, but I did not feel for one minute that I deserved the kind words it contained.

The thing that makes me very sad as I write this is that I never wrote Jimmy Carter a letter thanking him for taking the time to write such a beautiful letter for me. I didn't even pick up the phone and call him at the private number he provided to thank him.

It is easy to think that since a person is a former President of The United States and a winner of The Nobel Peace Prize they would not even notice a thank you letter from a person who has failed in as many respects as I did. But, that was reverse snobbery on my part. How bad I feel that I did not write Jimmy Carter and thank him for still another very kind thing that he had taken time away from his demanding schedule to do to help me.

I failed to be a good friend to Jimmy Carter in many ways. Now, it is too late for me to thank him for everything he did for me and to tell him that I love him. It is an empty feeling to write these things in this book, since I know that he will never get to read it.

However, I at least want people to know what a great person Jimmy Carter was in general and what a great friend he was to me in particular. I know that is the way that he would have treated every person who reads this book, if they had been fortunate enough to get to know him as I did. I pray that I will get to tell him how grateful I am to him and how much I love him in Heaven one day.

Life passes quickly by. President Carter is in hospice care right now as I type this. Miss Rosalynn has already passed away. My old friend, Jeff Carter, has been sick, too.

Another old friend of mine, Hamilton Jordon, died after fighting cancer for twenty years. So, I guess I am the only person left who knows the stories in this book.

If God will do a miracle and get this book published, I will be so thankful that I was at least able to let other people know what they would have learned about Jimmy Carter if they had been blessed to get to know him as I was.

# CHAPTER 23

## Getting to Know Congressman Brinkley

There was another prominent politician who also played a very big role in my life. He was U.S. Congressman Jack T. Brinkley of Columbus, Georgia.

I met Congressman Brinkley at the same Affirmation Vietnam Rally at Fort Valley High School at which I met Jimmy Carter. At that time, Brinkley was a member of the Georgia House of Representatives. He was considering running for the U. S. Congress that year. As it turned out, Jack Brinkley did get elected to Congress in 1966.

When Congressman Brinkley got to Washington, he and I stayed in close contact with each other. In 1967, when I was a junior in high school, I started getting invited to make speeches at civic clubs in towns from Macon to Columbus. This area included The Third Congressional District, which Congressman Brinkley had just started representing in Washington.

A man who lived around Pine Mountain heard me make a speech in his home town. He was a friend of my Daddy and owned a printing company. After hearing my speech, he said the he wanted to print it up in pamphlet form. I worked on the copy for it and he printed thousands of four page brochures based on the ideas I presented in my speech. I still have one of those brochures. The front page featured a drawing of The Statue of Liberty beside the outline of a map of the United States.

Somehow, Congressman Brinkley got one of these pamphlets. He had it inserted into The

Congressional Record and sent me copies of the pages of The Congressional Record that included my pamphlet. Naturally, this was very exciting to me.

Then, in 1968, I was the Attorney General of the Georgia Youth Assembly held at the State Capitol in Atlanta. As part of this job, I got to fly to Washington and meet some members of Georgia's Congressional delegation. Another member of the Youth Assembly came on this one-day trip with me.

We flew into The Baltimore-Washington International Airport, which is 32 miles northeast of Washington. I didn't know how we would get from there to Washington. But, when we got off the plane, we were met by two of Congressman Brinkley's staff members. He had sent them to pick us up and drive us to his office on Capitol Hill.

When we got to his office, Congressman Brinkley gave me a warm welcome. He and I really hit it off even more than we had before. He took my assistant and me on a tour of the Capitol. I still have a picture Congressman Brinkley had taken of us with him on the lawn in front of the Capitol.

Congressman Brinkley told me that other members of Congress from Georgia, including Senator Richard B. Russell, had asked him to bring me to their offices to meet them.

I remember my meeting with Senator Russell very well. He was very nice to me. After we talked about our mutual interest in history, he called his good friend, President Lyndon Johnson, to see if I could come to The White House and have my picture taken with him.

After we finished meeting members of the Georgia congressional delegation, we flew back to Atlanta. When we arrived at the large ballroom where all the members of the Youth Assembly were having their closing banquet, I was able to tell them how kind Congressman Brinkley had been to me on my trip to Washington.

When I went to bed that night, I thought about how exciting it had been for me to be on Capitol Hill that day. I prayed that, if it was God's will, I could work up there one day.

That was one of the greatest days in my 17-year old life. More importantly, it deepened and cemented my friendship with Congressman Brinkley.

# CHAPTER 24

## The Brinkley Advice Clubs

While I was still in high school, Congressman Brinkley offered me a very interesting job that I really enjoyed. He asked me to visit high schools in his district and organize interested students into what we called The Brinkley Advice Clubs or Congress Clubs.

The idea behind these clubs was the same idea that I had used when I set up Teenagers for Carter. We wanted to get young people involved with Congressman Brinkley. If they liked him, we knew they would tell their parents about his interest in them. We thought that, in addition to getting many young people involved in politics, this would also give their parents a good impression of Congressman Brinkley.

The clubs worked like this. From time to time, the members at each high school's club met and discussed political issues in which they were interested. Then, they voted to choose an issue they wanted to bring to Congressman Brinkley's attention. When the members of these clubs expressed an interest in any particular issue, I wrote a report to Congressman Brinkley telling him the advice these young people wanted to pass on to him.

These clubs were fun for students who were interested in politics and government. There was one suggestion the students in these clubs made to Congressman Brinkley that actually led to a policy change in Washington.

The students in these clubs had heard about something that was important to the soldiers from Georgia serving in Vietnam. The Brinkley Advice Clubs, or Congress Clubs, voted to ask Congressman Brinkley to look into the matter. I wrote Congressman Brinkley a report about this and sent it to him.

When Congressman Brinkley got my report, he immediately set out to change this policy. He was on the Armed Services Committee, so the military leaders wanted to cooperate with him in every way possible.

As a result, the Defense Department modified its rule. The soldiers from Georgia serving in Vietnam got the change they wanted.

Congressman Brinkley put a speech about this in The Congressional Record. It was a great feeling for the students in these clubs to know that they had made a real difference on behalf of all the soldiers from Georgia serving in Vietnam.

The students in these clubs had boosted the morale of Georgia's soldiers serving in Vietnam. They had also learned a lot about how our government and our political system work. Congressman Brinkley was very pleased with the results of these clubs.

# CHAPTER 25

## A Job I Loved

After graduating from college in 1972, I took a job working in the advertising department of The Bank of North Carolina, N.A. in the coastal town of Jacksonville, North Carolina. Before I took this job, I told the secretary of the draft board in Fort Valley that I was thinking about taking this job. But, I told her that I didn't want to do so, if I was going to be drafted.

She assured me that I would not be drafted, so Julie and I loaded our furniture on a moving van and moved. Sure enough, while the moving van was being unloaded at the apartment we had rented in Jacksonville, the mail man drove up and handed me my draft notice. I went and took my Army physical at Fort Bragg. After that, they told me that I should report to Fort Jackson in Columbia, South Carolina for basic training in March of 1973.

Julie and I continued to live in Jacksonville until it was time for me to report to Fort Jackson. I enjoyed working at the bank. But, during that same time, we found out that my Daddy had cancer.

While I was at basic training, I found out that Daddy's cancer was terminal. Because of this, Julie and I wanted to live much closer to Momma and Daddy in Fort Valley than we would have been if we had returned to Jacksonville, N.C. The problem was that I didn't have any idea of what job I could get when I finished my active duty training with the Army.

One day during lunch, I got an idea. I walked to the nearest pay phone and called Congressman Brinkley's office in Washington. Fortunately, he was in his office and told his secretary that he would talk with me. This was the first time I had talked with him since 1968, five years before. I had been afraid that he might not even remember who I was.

But, he did remember me, and he was very kind to me. I explained my situation to him. He listened carefully and told me to call him back the next day during my lunch break. When I called him the next day, he offered me a job being his Research Assistant and working out of his district office in Warner Robins, Georgia, which was only about thirty minutes from Fort Valley.

So, when I finished active duty training and was sent back to my Army Reserve unit in Fort Valley, Julie and I moved into an apartment in Warner Robins. My office was located in the Warner Robins City Hall, and I even had a secretary to work in that office with me.

I had always dreamed of being a Congressman, so I loved this job. The Warner Robins office was there primarily to help constituents with problems they had with government agencies. However, Congressman Brinkley sent me to visit people all over the district that he represented.

I also made talks at civic clubs, schools and other groups around the district. My secretary, an absolutely wonderful young lady named Sandy Jones, kept track of the speeches I made.

One year, I made over one hundred speeches on behalf of Congressman Brinkley. I also hosted a talk show on the Warner Robins cable TV channel. It was called "Value Search." On the show I discussed current events with a guest and took phone calls from the audience.

I loved everything about the job, and Julie and I loved living in Warner Robins. We could have been happy there forever. I would see Congressman Brinkley often and talk with him on the phone almost every day. We were getting along great.

Sadly, during this otherwise very happy time, my Daddy got sicker and sicker with cancer. Congressman Brinkley could see how devastated I was. He asked me if there was anything he could do to help me. I said, "Yes, sir, I wish you would introduce a bill requiring the federal government to set up a special agency with the same priority that NASA has to find a cure for cancer." To his immense credit, Congressman Brinkley did introduce such a bill.

He introduced the bill in time for me to tell my Daddy about it before he died. We knew that no cure would be found in time to help Daddy, but I wanted him to know that his suffering had resulted in an effort to make the government give the same priority to finding a cure for cancer that it had given to putting men on the moon.

Congressman Brinkley and I worked very hard on this bill. He had other people on his staff do a lot of research on the existing state of the government's efforts to find a cure for cancer. He discovered that the government had many credible proposals that could hold a key to eliminating this horrible disease. However, they were not being pursued because the government would not fund them. This made Congressman Brinkley redouble his efforts on the Brinkley Cancer Bill, as it became known.

During this time, my Daddy died of cancer. Congressman Brinkley came to his funeral. After the funeral, he and I talked about Daddy and the cancer bill. He could see how distraught I was. He asked me to write a letter that he could send to every other member of Congress about why his cancer bill should be passed.

I made this my top priority. Part of the letter I proposed included the likelihood that at least one member of every American family would get cancer during their lifetime. The other big argument we made was that, if the government could spend vast amounts of money to send a handful of Americans to the moon, it should surely be willing to spend a similar amount of money to save all Americans from the possibility of getting cancer.

Congressman Brinkley made a wonderful speech in support of his cancer bill on the floor of the House of Representatives. However, it did not get the support it needed to pass. The reason for its defeat was that it would be too expensive to find a cure for cancer. Nobody questioned what Congressman Brinkley had discovered, that the government had many promising proposals from scientists and doctors that might lead to progress in the fight against cancer, if the government would just fund them.

I could not believe that the United States Congress thought sending a few people to the moon was more important than ending cancer. That was sad. But, it was wonderful that Congressman Brinkley had the courage to fight so hard for this bill, which had been inspired by Daddy's suffering. Even though it did not pass, it did result in a lot of new information coming to light about the inadequacy of our government's funding of the fight against cancer.

There were several times while I was working for Congressman Brinkley in Warner Robins when he asked me to come to Washington for a few days. Whenever I had a break during those visits, I would go sit in the gallery of the House or Senate chambers. It was so wonderful to me. I would look down at Congressmen or Senators talking with each other on the House or Senate floor and just wonder what it would feel like to be one of them. I knew that was what I wanted to do with my life. But, there is no greater distance than the distance from working for a Congressman or Senator to being one. It was a journey that I would never get to take.

The years that Julie and I lived in Warner Robins and I worked for Congressman Brinkley in his office there were some of the happiest days of our life together. It was all possible because Congressman Brinkley remembered me from my days in high school and went far out of his way to help Julie and me when we were desperate to find a place to live and a job after I got out of the active duty phase of my time in the Army Reserve.

# CHAPTER 26

## A Terrible Misunderstanding

In 1975, I had a talk with Congressman Brinkley about my future. I told him that Julie was going to have a baby and that we were ready to buy a house in Warner Robins. I asked him if he had any plans to move me to Washington. He said that he intended to keep me in Warner Robins, and that we should feel secure about buying the house we had selected.

I'm positive that Congressman Brinkley was absolutely sincere in what he told me. He was one of the best friends I ever had in my life. Even though we went through some rocky times, our friendship never ended. It stayed strong and eventually brought us back together again.

But, one day in 1975, I got a strange call from my friend, Larry Wheeler, who was Congressman Brinkley's Administrative Assistant in Washington. He was very friendly, as he always was. He said, "You know, Steve, every ship can only have one captain." I said, "I know Larry. That's surely true." He didn't explain what he meant, and I didn't think it was important enough to ask him what he meant.

We both could have handled that phone call a lot better. If we had just talked about what was really on Congressman Brinkley's mind, a lot of unpleasant drama could have been very easily prevented.

It turned out that a longtime supporter of Congressman Brinkley in Warner Robins told him that I was planning to run against him in 1976. He based this on the fact that I was making so many speeches and hosting that TV show. In my mind, I was doing my job of helping Congressman Brinkley by doing these things. I thought that if I made a speech and people liked me, it would make them like Congressman Brinkley more, because I was speaking as a member of his staff.

I always had a dream of one day being a Congressman, but running against Congressman Brinkley had never even crossed my mind. I was very happy working for him in Warner Robins. It was the best of both worlds. I was involved with politics and working for a Congressman, but I got to live in a small city and spend a lot of time with Julie.

Not long after Larry called me, I got a call from Congressman Brinkley. He offered me a promotion. He wanted me to move to Washington and be the Counsel for a subcommittee of which he had just become Chairman. It would have included a substantial increase in my salary, and it would have been fun for me to be right in the thick of things on Capitol Hill.

However, it didn't add up to me. Not long before, Congressman Brinkley had assured me that he was going to keep me in my job in Warner Robins. Because of that, Julie and I had bought a house. We were very happy, and Julie was expecting our first child. I told all of this to Congressman Brinkley. I said, "I appreciate the offer, Congressman, but I want to keep my job working for you in Warner Robins."

Congressman Brinkley then made some suggestions to address my concerns. He said that I could fly with him from to Washington every Tuesday morning and fly back to Georgia with him every Thursday night, so that way Julie and I could keep our house in Warner Robins. I would just be working in Washington three days a week and in Warner Robins the other two. I told him I appreciated that, but that I didn't want to be separated from Julie for three days a week.

However, I had begun to feel like Congressman Brinkley's main reason for offering me a job in Washington was to get me out of Warner Robins. So, I declined the job he had offered me in Washington. He told me that I could not keep working for him in Warner Robins. That meant I was fired.

The tragedy of the situation is that we never discussed or even mentioned what was behind all this. Congressman Brinkley did not tell me that he believed I was going to run against him in1976, and I didn't have the maturity to even ask him why he no longer wanted me to work for him in Warner Robins. If we had discussed what was on his mind, I could have quickly assured him that I had no intention whatsoever of ever running against him and that I would be happy to quit making speeches and give up my TV show, if he wanted me to do so. But, our conversation never got to the real issue.

This situation was a good example of how much I missed the guidance my Daddy had always given me. If Daddy had been alive, I would have told him what Congressman Brinkley had told me, and I am sure he would have told me how to handle the situation in a way that would have kept me working for Congressman Brinkley. I never knew how much I had relied on my Daddy until after he died. For his part, Congressman Brinkley could have told me that he had been told that I was planning to run against him in 1976, and the whole matter could have been easily resolved.

Congressman Brinkley told me years later that he had gotten some very bad advice that led to that situation. The truth is that we both let the situation get blown way out of hand. I regret that very much, and I know Congressman Brinkley did, too. But, as you will see, we did eventually end up back together again.

# CHAPTER 27

## A Regrettable Mistake

After Congressman Brinkley fired me, I got offered a job being a lender at a bank in Warner Robins. It was a good job, and I have often wished that I had kept it until I reached retirement age.

There was just one problem. I hated it. Sitting there all day long, asking person after person the same questions to determine if they could qualify for a loan was just not something I enjoyed.

I used to keep a legal pad on my desk and divide the entire work day into fifteen minute blocks. Then, throughout the day, I would check off every fifteen minutes that went by.

One day the President of the bank called me into his office. He said, "You know, I think a person's priorities should be God first, their family second, and the bank third. But, I don't even think the bank makes your Top Ten!"

Still, I was determined to make a career of banking. Then, one night in early 1976, I got a phone call from Mack Mattingly. He was the Chairman of the Republican Party of Georgia. Later, he would be elected as the first Republican Senator from Georgia since reconstruction.

He had heard about me being fired by Congressman Brinkley. He said the Republican Party needed a candidate for Congress from our district in that year's election. He said that, if I would run, the Republican Party would provide me with the money I needed to wage a competitive campaign and a campaign manager to help me.

I was going to turn 26 in May of that year, so I would have been old enough to serve if I had gotten elected. I had always dreamed of being a member of Congress. I thought it was my destiny. So, I told him that I would do it.

Soon thereafter, I left the bank and campaigned for Congress full time. I let my heart make that decision, not my brain. That style of decision making has gotten me in trouble all my life. It was another mistake that I would never have made if my Daddy had still been alive.

I did not like the idea of running against Congressman Brinkley. But, I honestly thought I would make a great Congressman. I still believe that.

But, looking back on it, I know that I made a terrible, immature, disloyal and egotistical decision. I also found out something about myself. While I was great at campaigning for people that I believed in, like Jimmy Carter and Jack Brinkley, I was horrible at campaigning for myself.

My speeches were very good. But, most of the campaigning done every day was one-on-one meetings with voters. I had seen Carter and Brinkley do it so well, but I was terrible at it. I think it was because I didn't have the self-confidence necessary to promote myself.

In the middle of the campaign, I had a meeting in Columbus with a group of about ten major Republican contributors. At this meeting, they showed me a full page ad they had bought to run in the following Sunday's Columbus Ledger-Inquirer.

The headline of the ad read "Jack Brinkley Has Failed."

I told them that they could not run that ad, because I did not think Congressman Brinkley had failed. I told them that I liked Congressman Brinkley and would not let them use my campaign to attack him.

They then said that, if I didn't let them run the ad, they would not contribute to my campaign. I responded that, while I needed their contributions, I would not let them run that newspaper advertisement.

I felt that these big donor Republicans were not interested in promoting me as a candidate. I thought they mainly wanted to use my campaign to attack Congressman Brinkley and weaken his image, so that a stronger Republican candidate could beat him in the next election two years later.

I already felt bad enough running against Congressman Brinkley, but I wasn't going to be a party to attacking a person that I knew was a good man. I was running because I really thought I would be a great Congressman, not because I thought Congressman Brinkley had not done a good job. I just thought I could do a better one.

What I did not know was that one of the people at that meeting posing as a Republican donor was a good friend of Congressman Brinkley. He told Congressman Brinkley what had happened at that meeting.

I think that was one of the things that saved my friendship with Jack Brinkley. Politicians don't know who they can trust, because so many people want to use them. But, when two people run against each other and they both treat the other one fairly, they come out of the campaign knowing they can trust the other one.

One night during the campaign, the Georgia Public Television system invited Congressman Brinkley and me to have a debate. We both agreed to participate. During the debate, one of the news reporters asked me if I was worried about the way my campaign was going.

I said, "No, because, if God wants me to win, I will win. And, if He doesn't want me to win, I'll be better off losing. But, regardless of whether Congressman Brinkley or I win, I know our district will have a good Congressman next year."

Years later, Congressman Brinkley told me that was the only time he had been afraid he might lose the election. "When you said that if God wanted you to win, then you would win," he told me, "I thought yes, if God wants him to win, he will win."

After that debate ended and everyone had left the auditorium at Columbus College, where it was held, Congressman Brinkley asked me to meet with him privately in a room behind the stage.

He was extremely nice. He asked me how Julie and I were doing. Then, he put his arm around my shoulders and said, "You're doing a great job. I'm very proud of you."

On Friday, October 22, 1976, which was about two weeks before the election, *The Atlanta Constitution* published an interview with me about my campaign. It was written by Claudia Townsend of the paper's Washington Bureau.

The headline above the article read, "Third District Race Is Clean." Ms. Townsend said that although I knew that I would almost certainly lose the election, I had told her that I thought the campaign had done me some good.

"I could go anywhere in these 17 counties and have a flat tire, and I'd have a friend nearby to call now. I've made a lot of friends and learned a lot of lessons, and if I'm not elected, I'll have an awful lot of benefits from having run," she quoted me as having told her.

By that time, Congressman Brinkley had raised about $40,000 for his campaign. I had raised about

$10,000. I had also received much less money from the Republican Party than the other Republican candidates in Georgia that year.

I only received $500 from the Republican Party. But, I told Ms. Townsend that "I've decided not to worry about the help I don't get, but to be grateful for the help I do get."

She quoted Congressman Brinkley's campaign manager as saying, "Steve is an astute young man; he's got a lot to offer. It's a shame he didn't start at some other level." She was surely right about that.

Ms. Townsend wrote that I had been forced by my limited budget to rely primarily on a person-to-person style of campaigning. That's not a bad thing to do, but you do need more money than I had to support your person-to-person campaigning with more advertising than I could afford.

I did purchase thirty minutes of TV time to air a program the night before the election. I even invited Congressman Brinkley to come on that program and discuss the issues with me.

In the letter I wrote to him inviting him to do that, I told him, "I suggest confining the subjects to be discussed to assure you that I have no intention of using the night before the election to make any political criticism of you." However Congressman Brinkley wrote me back declining to be on the program, saying "It is not possible to rearrange my schedule to fit yours." I understood his position. At that point, he was so far ahead that he had nothing to gain from debating me. If I had been in his position, I probably would have done the same thing.

Earlier in the campaign, Congressman Brinkley and I had appeared on four programs together. During those joint appearances, Congressman

Brinkley emphasized his record and stressed that his position on The Armed Services Committee enabled him to protect Fort Benning and Robins Air Force Base, two huge military bases in the district. He was right to do that.

In those appearances, I did not attack Congressman Brinkley. Instead, I attacked the overall dysfunction of the entire Congress. My point was that he was doing a good job on individual issues, but he had not done anything to change the fact that Congress as a whole was creating more problems than it solved.

"I've been talking about the need for real realistic leadership in Washington," I said. "Politicians are reluctant to realistically confront the tough issues." As an example of my willingness to face difficult issues, I said that "I would favor reinstituting the draft and deregulating the price of natural gas."

"Our generation, people in their 20's and 30's, know that if we don't adopt some realistic policies in Washington soon, we're going to live through the disasters that a failure to be realistic is going to bring," I was quoted as saying.

Ms. Townsend's article concluded by saying that I had avoided personal attacks on Congressman Brinkley, even though such attacks were being made in other Congressional races.

"I realize I might not win," I told her, "but what I can do is have a campaign I can be proud of for the rest of my life. It's up to the voters to decide whether I win, but it's up to me whether I have a good, decent campaign."

I had made a terrible mistake by running for Congress. I realized that in the middle of the campaign. But, at least I didn't resort to personal attacks like many politicians do. I am thankful that

God led me to handle inevitable defeat as well as I could.

Once you buy a ticket on the Titanic and the ship sails out into the open ocean, you can't jump off and swim back to shore. But, you can try to conduct yourself as well as possible when it hits an iceberg. That's what I tried to do.

Well, as I've said, my campaign had almost no money to spend. But, I kept campaigning as best I could until Election Day. Very early that night, the TV stations declared that Congressman Brinkley had won easily.

It turned out that he got 93,174 votes which was 88.7%. I got 11,829 votes or 11.3%. It was the most one-sided result in all the Congressional elections in the United States that year, except for one race in which I heard the losing candidate had been in federal prison during the campaign and on Election

Day. After that election, my favorite saying was, "11,829 Georgians can't be wrong!"

I remember staying up all night on election night to watch the Presidential election results come in on TV. The national TV networks covered the Presidential election for the first 25 minutes of every half hour. For the last five minutes of every half hour, the local stations gave the local results. I would jump up when the local results were coming on to turn off the sound on the TV. I didn't want to keep hearing about how badly I had done.

I was very happy early the next morning when President Ford conceded the Presidential election to Jimmy Carter. I wondered about what Jimmy Carter must have thought when he looked at his ballot when he voted and saw my name listed as the Republican candidate to be his Congressman. I imagine he felt sorry for me.

Only two people called me to console me on the day after the election. One was my mother. The other was Congressman Brinkley. He could not have been nicer. I called the President of the bank and asked if he would give me my job back. He emphatically said that he would not.

The following Saturday I went to Grant Field in Atlanta to watch my beloved Georgia Tech Yellow Jackets play eleventh ranked Notre Dame.

In a big upset, Tech won 23 to 14. The Yellow Jackets did not even attempt a pass in the entire game. The next day at church, our preacher asked me how I was doing. I said, "Well, I got clobbered on Tuesday, but Tech beat Notre Dame yesterday. So, on balance, I would say it was a pretty good week." The truth was, however, that the week had left me with no job and no future in politics.

The real hero of the election turned out to be my wife, Julie. I had made a horrible mistake that had placed her and our two boys in a terrible situation. However, Julie never criticized me about it. She could not have been more loving and supportive.

When her Daddy asked me how I was going to take care of my family after that election, all I could say was that I was going to trust God. It didn't seem like much of a plan at the time, but I have learned during my life that trusting God is always the best plan anybody can have.

# CHAPTER 28

## The Prodigal Son Returns

After this shellacking, almost nobody would hire me. They told me they were afraid that Congressman Brinkley would be mad with them, if they did. Finally, when I was about to give up on finding a job, I went to see a man I knew who was the manager of a rock and roll radio station.

He said he had not even heard about the election. He might have been kidding about that but, thank the Lord, he gave me a job selling radio ads for his station. I did not like rock and roll, and I did not know anything about it. But, this was the man who had been willing to hire me, and I was determined to do everything I could to do a good job.

Every morning, I would get to my little office at the station and read a book of Proverbs and five Psalms. Then I would look at the previous day's *Warner Robins Daily Sun* and that morning's *Macon Telegraph*. Then, I made a list of every store in Warner Robins that had an advertisement in either one of those newspapers.

After that, I got in my car and went to see all these people who had placed advertisements in those papers. It was tough going, but somehow God caused enough people to buy radio ads to keep us going. It was a miracle.

I liked the people at the radio station. I also liked making friends with a lot of merchants I had not known before. Everybody I contacted was very nice to me. But, I knew that my future probably did not lie in rock and roll.

Therefore, I applied to the Mercer University Law School in Macon. I got accepted but could not begin until the fall of 1977.

While I had made a terrible mistake in running for Congress and had become almost unemployable in the process, God was still working out his plan for my life. If I hadn't lost the election so badly, I might have been able to get my job back at the bank or find another long-term job. If I had, I would have never gone to law school. But, since I did go to law school, I had an opportunity later in my life to work at an interesting job and to try to help a lot of people who needed a lawyer.

During the three years while I was attending law school, three things happened that helped rebuild my relationship with Congressman Brinkley.

First, a few days before Thanksgiving every year I was in law school, Congressman Brinkley sent his son, Fred, from Columbus to our house in Warner Robins with a big turkey for us to have for our Thanksgiving dinner. Years later, Fred and I became very close friends and fishing buddies. We would go fishing together two or three times every week.

Second, I saw that somebody had written a very critical letter about Congressman Brinkley to the editor of *The Columbus Ledger-Enquirer*. The paper printed this person's letter. I knew the letter was unfair and untrue. So, I wrote a letter to the paper setting the record straight and standing up for Congressman Brinkley, which the paper also printed. My friend Larry Wheeler, who was Congressman Brinkley's Administrative Assistant in Washington, called me and told me how much my letter had meant to Congressman Brinkley. That made me very happy.

Third, I got a call during my third year of law school from Mr. Jim Blanchard, the President of The Columbus Bank and Trust Company in Columbus. He said that a charity roast of Congressman Brinkley was being planned. He asked me if I would like to come and be the "mystery roaster," which meant that nobody would know in advance that I was going to be taking part in the program. I told him that I would love to do it.

The roast was a formal affair held in the beautiful Springer Opera House in downtown Columbus. First opened in 1871, this beautiful theatre was named The State Theatre of Georgia by Governor Jimmy Carter on its 100th anniversary in 1971.

My approach to public speaking is to not prepare and instead to be guided about what to say by the feeling I get from the audience. Using this method,

I have made some very good speeches and some absolutely horrible ones.

I really wanted this speech to be good. But, as I sat in a private room back stage waiting to be introduced, I was panicking. I had just not been able to think of anything to say. I could hear Senator Herman Talmadge making his speech, and I had been told that I would be called out right after Senator Talmadge finished.

The organizers of the event had asked a member of the Columbus Jaycees to stay with me in the little room where I was waiting. Right before I was supposed to go on, this young man said to me, "Are you going to run again?" I thought that, considering how badly I had gotten beaten when I ran, this young man's question was the most hilarious thing I had ever heard in my life. Just then, I heard loud applause coming from inside the theatre. I knew that meant I was going to be called out right away.

The next thing I heard was Mr. Jim Blanchard introducing the mystery speaker. He said, "Now, here he is, Jack's favorite opponent, Steve Dugan!"

When I walked out onto the stage to the podium, I was standing right beside where Congressman Brinkley was sitting. We looked at each other and smiled.

I started my speech by saying this, "I was a little discouraged after that last election but, after hearing all these objective remarks about Congressman Brinkley and his career, I've decided I'm going to run again!" That got a big laugh. After that God made one great story after another pop into my head.

My favorite one was this one. "After the election, I read in the newspaper that Congressman Brinkley's campaign manager was going to throw a big banquet for him and all his supporters. So, I called my campaign manager, Edward Swearingen of Reynolds, Georgia, and asked him if he would throw a supper for me and all my supporters. He said, 'I sure will.' I said, 'How soon can you do it?' He said, 'As soon as I can shoot a rabbit!'"

I don't know where these stories came from. I think they must have come from God, But, when I finished by sharing with the crowd how encouraging Congressman Brinkley had been to me during and after our election campaign, I got a thunderous standing ovation from the crowd led by Congressman Brinkley, himself. I looked at him and he had a big smile on his face. I knew God had fully restored my friendship with this wonderful man.

When we got back to our hotel after the program was over, our phone rang. It was Congressman Brinkley asking me to go to a breakfast meeting with him the next morning. I told him I would love to do it, but that I hadn't brought a regular suit to Columbus, just the tuxedo I had worn to the program. He said, "Don't worry. I'll have Fred bring you one of his suits to your hotel. You can wear it."

So, the next morning I showed up in a suit that didn't come close to fitting. But, that didn't matter. Congressman Brinkley and I had a wonderful reunion.

I have always been so thankful to God that He let me make a good speech that night. I think it was the best speech I ever made, and the most important.

# CHAPTER 29

## Another Job I Loved

In the spring of 1980, I was within a few months of graduating from law school. I started trying to find a job. While I had been in law school, I had worked as a clerk for a lawyer in Warner Robins. He and his family were extremely nice to me. However, he had a daughter who was in law school, and I wasn't sure how long he might have a place for me in his office.

So, I went around visiting lawyers in Warner Robins looking for a job. I thought that after three years of law school people would have forgotten about the election and that I would be able to find a job. But, it turned out that I was wrong.

Many of the lawyers I talked with said they would not hire me because they were afraid of alienating Congressman Brinkley. By that time, Julie and I had two little boys and a big student loan to start repaying. I began to get worried. I was about to graduate from law school, and I could not find a job.

I was very discouraged and afraid. But, one day I got a hand written letter from Congressman Brinkley. I still remember my hands shaking as I opened it. In it, he said he wanted me to come to Washington as soon as I finished law school and be his Legislative Assistant.

It was very unusual for any politician to hire a person who had worked for him before and then run against him. I had not asked Congressman Brinkley to give me another job or told him of the problem I was having finding a job. But, somehow, he decided to do it.

I have almost never been happier about anything in my life than I was when I got that letter. I had gone from almost giving up on ever getting any job to getting the greatest job I could imagine.

To me, it was both a tribute to Congressman Brinkley's character and a miracle from God. I put that letter under the glass on the top of our dresser. Every day I looked at it and thanked God for the miracle of getting that job with Congressman Brinkley.

The day after I graduated from Mercer Law School, Julie, our two little boys, and I moved to Alexandria, Virginia. Then, I started working for Congressman Brinkley in The Rayburn House Office Building.

Congressman Brinkley knew how much I had wanted to be a Congressman. And, he did everything he could to make my experience on his staff as much like being a Congressman as possible.

I would get to the office very early every morning. The first thing I would do was to look at the list of bills that were going to be voted on that day. That list would only have been decided on late the night before by the Speaker and the Democratic leadership team.

Next, I would type up an index card for each bill. On this card, I would type the bill number, a summary of the bill, comments Congressman Brinkley had received from constituents about it, and a recommendation to Congressman Brinkley about how he should vote on the bill.

When I had prepared an index card for every bill that was going to be voted on that day, I would hand all the index cards to Congressman Brinkley. He would put them in his inside coat pocket and refer to them as the votes on the bills came up during the day.

After that, I would be given all the mail regarding legislation and politics that had come into the office that morning. My job was to prepare a response to each letter and have it typed for Congressman Brinkley to review and sign, if he approved it. He got a lot of mail about legislation and politics every day, so preparing the answers took a lot of my time.

Usually in the late afternoon, Congressman Brinkley would call me to come into his office or meet him in the cloak room right off the House floor to go over the letters he had received that day and the responses I had prepared for his consideration and signature. He would sign some of the answers I had prepared and tell me to change some others.

Then, I would give the ones he had signed to my secretary to be mailed and dictate new letters to replace the ones he had told me to change. Once the revised letters were typed, I would take them to him to review and sign. After that, they would be mailed.

Finally, each letter received and a copy of each letter mailed in response was filed. In addition, the incoming and outgoing letters were noted on a file card that was kept in a filing system used to document every contact Congressman Brinkley had with his constituents.

Congressman Brinkley carefully maintained that file card system. Because he did, he could quickly look at one card and become familiar with every time he had communicated with that person during all the years he had been in Congress.

Congressman Brinkley was famous for his excellent memory of constituents and their interests. He did have a great memory, but he also had a great system to back it up. There is an art to being a successful politician, and Congressman Brinkley had mastered it.

Handling legislative and political mail was extremely important to Congressman Brinkley, and he had some strict rules about it. First, an answer to every letter had to be sent out on the same day the letter was received. Second, all reply letters I prepared for him to sign could only be one page long. Third, the letters had to be perfectly typed and centered on the page. He felt like the appearance of a letter was just as important as it content.

Throughout the day, I would dictate answers to the legislative and political letters Congressman Brinkley received and hand my dictation tapes to the secretary he had assigned to me. Then, she would type them as I dictated answers to some more.

Another part of my job was to take all the calls regarding legislation or politics that Congressman

Brinkley received during the day and prepare a summary sheet for each call. At the end of the day, he would call me into his office to go over the call sheets and sit with him while he returned the calls.

I arranged the call sheets of the legislative and political calls he had received during the day in the order of how important I thought they were. I remember one day when I learned a big lesson from him about politics.

On that day, Congressman Brinkley had received fourteen phone calls about legislation and politics. Thirteen of them were from constituents I had never heard of scattered throughout the district. The other one was from President Reagan. Naturally, I put the one from President Reagan on the top of the stack.

When I handed the call sheets to Congressman Brinkley, he put the sheet with the call from President Reagan at the bottom of the stack. Then, he began returning the calls he had received from constituents. He talked with them in a friendly and informal way, patiently listening to everything they wanted to tell him.

After he had returned the calls from about six constituents, I could not stand it anymore. I said, "Congressman, don't you think you should return the President's call?" He said, "Why?" I said, "There could be a war starting or something like that."

Congressman Brinkley looked at me with a smile and said, "There's no war. If there were a war, the President wouldn't have time to talk to me. He wants my vote on some bill that's coming up. But, I want the votes of these thirteen constituents. So, I will call all of them back first."

Of course, Congressman Brinkley was absolutely right. He used to end all his speeches in the district by saying, "I promise to always remember who I am, where I'm from, and who sent me." The way he handled those phone calls was a perfect example of how closely he kept that promise.

Another job Congressman Brinkley assigned to me was to go in his place on what were officially called "fact finding missions." Unofficially, the media referred to them as "junkets."

By the time I got to Washington, Congressman Brinkley had become the Chairman of the House Armed Services Committee's Subcommittee on Military Installations and Facilities. This meant that every time the military wanted the money to improve or expand a military base, their request had to go before Congressman Brinkley's subcommittee.

One day, Congressman Brinkley called me to come into his office. When I walked in, I saw that there were two military officers sitting with him.

He introduced them to me. Then, he said, "These men want me to go on special trips to see military bases all over the United States and the world. I have told them that I do not have the time to go on these trips, and that I am going to be sending you in my place."

After that, I was sent on a lot of very interesting trips. On a day when a trip was scheduled to begin, the members of Congress or their assistants going on the trip would gather at the horseshoe entrance to the Rayburn Building.

Then, a military bus would pick us up and take us to Andrews Air Force Base, where we would board one of those special jets with the same insignia and coloring as Air Force One. I was surprised to learn that there was a whole fleet of those planes.

Within minutes, we would be on our way. It was always a big thrill for me to go to Andrews Air Force

Base and get on one of those planes that looked like Air Force One.

I was having a great time getting to do a job I loved, thanks to God and Congressman Brinkley. It was the only job I ever had that I liked so much that I almost dreaded the weekends.

# Chapter 30

## Fact Finding Missions

The "fact finding missions" Congressman Brinkley sent me on were organized by the military branches to show members of Congress or members of their staffs projects at military installations for which Congressional support was needed. The military branches had liaison offices in the Rayburn House Office Building. Officers working in these offices coordinated all Congressional relations.

I always felt that the military did not really understand how Congress worked. I came to this conclusion based on the fact that, while I was on these fact finding missions, they really seemed to think my opinion mattered. If they just knew how insignificant I was, I'm sure they would have never taken me on these inspection tours.

The military spared no effort in trying to make a good impression on Congress. I remember one trip I was on to The Aberdeen Proving Ground in Maryland. This trip was different from every other one in which I participated, because The Speaker of The House of Representatives, Tip O'Neill, was in the small group on the trip.

The Speaker's presence meant there were two ambulances following our busses and extra doctors on the trip. We also had the best police escort you could imagine.

It was a cold, stormy day. We boarded busses in the horseshoe of The Rayburn House Office Building and went to Andrews Air Force Base. When we got there, we got on helicopters for the short trip to The Aberdeen Proving Ground.

I remember that the Army wanted to demonstrate the effectiveness of a new tank that was being tested. I can still see the huge testing area that was constructed to test this new tank's ability to maneuver at high speed across rough terrain, up and down steep hills, and across rivers and streams.

For some reason, the military wanted a few people from Congress who were on the trip to ride in a tank as it went through this long, rugged obstacle course. I was selected to ride in one of the tanks being tested. I guess the Army thought that compared to Tip O'Neill and the other Congressmen on the trip, I was completely expendable.

When I got in this tank, I did not know what to expect. I did notice that there were razor sharp unpadded pieces of steel near to where I was told to stand or sit in the tank.

When the tank started its run across the large obstacle course, it was going very fast. I was being shaken around by the varying terrain features the tank was challenging throughout the test.

I kept looking at the exposed pieces of sharp steel about even with my neck around the hatch of the tank. I was never very coordinated. I had slipped or fallen many times in much less challenging positions than this. I thought, "These people have not thought this through! I'm going to slip and get beheaded. Why in the world am I in this tank?"

Finally the ride was over, and I emerged from the tank. The test may have made a good impression on Speaker O'Neill and the other Congressmen on the trip who watched the test.

But, if anybody had asked me for my opinion, I would not have had too many favorable things to say about the people who organized the test or the safety of the tank. Fortunately for the Army, nobody asked me for my opinion. In fact, nobody ever asked me for my opinion about anything I saw on these fact finding missions.

After we had finished at The Aberdeen Proving Ground, we were flown by helicopter to a beautiful, large clubhouse on Chesapeake Bay. When we went into the room that had been prepared for us, we were given a wonderful meal.

I had never eaten oysters, but everybody raved about them. So, I gave them a try. I knew pretty quickly that I had made a mistake in eating the oysters, but I hoped I would not let it show until I got home.

While we were there, all forty of us on the trip had a chance to meet the famous author James A. Michener. He was sitting at a table in the large room to sign copies of his book *Chesapeake*. I asked him to sign a copy to my wife, Julie, and he did. He was very kind to me.

When we finished there, we boarded the helicopters again to fly back to Washington. Helicopter rides are never smooth and by then the weather had gotten very bad. I was sitting by the famous lawyer, Edward Bennett Williams. He had owned the Washington Redskins and served as treasurer of Democratic National Committee. At the time of this trip, he owned the Baltimore Orioles baseball team.

At the start of that day, Mr. Williams did not have any idea who I was. However, I am afraid that he never forgot me. The combination of the rough helicopter ride and the disagreeability of the oysters was too much for me to handle. I'm afraid that Mr. Williams never wore that pair of shoes again.

Another "fact finding mission" also stands out in my mind. On this one, our group of Congressmen and staffers flew to four major military installations.

The customary procedure on these visits was that we would be shown whatever the military wanted us to see. After that, we would have a meeting with the commanding officer of the military installation we were visiting.

I enjoyed these trips and wanted the military to know I was interested and paying close attention, in the hope that would cause the officers running the trips to invite me on more of them. So, I always asked an easy question to the commanding officer.

When we finished our inspection of Fort Sill, Oklahoma, I asked the commanding General what he would like to do more than anything else. He was a tough man in an immaculate uniform. He quickly replied, "Kill Boris!"

After our inspection of Fort Lewis, Washington, which had the tallest tress I had ever seen, I asked its tough commanding officer the same question. His answer was also, "Kill Boris!"

Next, we visited Fort Irwin, California. Another impressive and immaculately dressed commander gave me the same answer, "Kill Boris!"

The last installation we visited on that trip was Fort Ord, California. It is located on beautiful Monterey Bay, nestled between the Pacific Ocean and majestic mountains. I thought it was the most magnificent location I had ever seen.

When we finished our inspection of it, a General came into a room to speak with us. His shirt-tail was not fully tucked in, his hat was not resting exactly straight on his head, and his shoes did not look quite as spit shined as those of the other commanders we had talked with on that trip.

By then, I was getting alarmed by hearing high ranking military officers declare their fondest desire was to "Kill Boris!" So, I changed my question a little.

I said, "General, if we could go back to Washington and get you anything you wanted for your fort, what would you ask us for?" Without missing a beat, he replied, "Cable television."

I wrote down his name. I thought, "If Congressman Brinkley ever asks me 'Who was the most impressive military commander you met on that trip?', I'm going to give him this man's name. He's the only one who thinks like I do."

# Chapter 31

## My Dream Came True

I always loved history, and I couldn't have asked to be around more of it. It was thrilling to me to have a job that took me to Capitol Hill every day.

The Rayburn House Office Building is four floors tall. But, underneath it there are three levels of underground parking spaces, a basement, and a sub-basement.

Under the building, there is a tunnel system providing subway transportation to the Capitol and other buildings on Capitol Hill. There are also all types of shops and a restaurant. There is even a barbershop.

One time while I was getting a haircut, there was a prominent member of Congress getting his haircut in the chair beside mine. The chairs were separated by partitions, but I could see him in the mirror that ran all the way down the wall of the barbershop.

That very famous Congressman had three staff members with him. They debated over every single hair that the barber wanted to cut off his head. It was hilarious to me. One day, I saw the same man taking a sunbath on a hidden portion of the Capitol roof outside the House cloak room between votes. I was never able to take him seriously after those two incidents.

Every now and then, Congressman Brinkley would ask me to meet him in the member's dining room in the Capitol for lunch. These were exciting occasions for me. After we had lunch, we would take the subway back to the Rayburn Building and walk to our office.

One day after we had lunch in the Capitol and were walking back to the office, I told him how much his letter offering me the job of being his Legislative Assistant had meant to me. I told him I especially appreciated the fact that he had taken the time to both write the letter and address the envelope by hand.

Congressman Brinkley got a big smile on his face. He said, "Well, Dugan, I wouldn't feel too good about that. The only reason I wrote it by hand was that nobody in my office would type it for me!" I guess he had been quicker to forgive me for running against him than his staff had been!

Still, everybody who worked for Congressman Brinkley was very nice to me. His Administrative Assistant, Larry Wheeler, and I were very good friends. Larry lived in Alexandria too, so we often road to and from work together.

At lunch time, Larry and I would often go to a putting green and driving range across the pond from The Jefferson Memorial. Larry was a great golfer, and we always had a lot of fun.

I had to take the subway under the building to the Capitol several times every day. I could feel the historical importance of every part of the building. The original home of The House of Representatives was where Statuary Hall is now located.

But, my favorite part of the Capitol was the basement of the original building. That is where the United States Senate Chamber was located from 1810 to 1859, except for a five year period after the British destroyed it when they burned the Capitol during the War of 1812.

Interestingly, the United States Supreme Court met in this same room from 1860 until 1935. So, it is almost impossible to comprehend how much of American history was made in this one room, and how many great Americans served our country there.

I used to go and stand reverently at the entrance to this room, which is now called the "Old Senate Chamber." Usually there was no one else around as I looked at the desks where so many people I had studied about had spent so much of their time. I could literally feel their presence in that place, which was preserved to look just as it had when the Senate met there.

Since I was a little boy, it had been my dream to work in our nation's historic Capitol. Now, thanks to God and Congressman Brinkley, my dream had come true.

# CHAPTER 32

## The Telephone Call Caper

Around noon one Friday, Congressman Brinkley called me into his office. He told me that there was one constituent he was having an especially hard time dealing with. He said the man had called him with a complaint that was so ridiculous that he was afraid he would lose his patience if he had to talk with him.

"You're good at talking with people," he told me. "I've got to drive back to Columbus this afternoon, so I want you to go home right now, relax, and call this man for me. Then, call me and let me know how the call went, and you can have the rest of the day off."

That sounded like a great deal to me. I hated being stuck in traffic trying to get onto The Woodrow

Wilson Bridge during rush hour. By getting to go home in the middle of the day, I wouldn't have to go through that.

So, I took the information Congressman Brinkley gave me about this man and drove to Alexandria. When I got home, I went to where we had our only phone. It was located on the kitchen wall.

I thought this would be quick and easy. I called the man, told him Congressman Brinkley had asked me to call him, and started talking with him. The Congressman had been right. This man started criticizing Congressman Brinkley in a very inaccurate and unfair way.

I tried to reason with him, but the call just went from bad to worse. After thirty minutes of trying to be patient, I lost my composure. I hung up on the man and then ripped our telephone off the wall.

With no telephone, I couldn't call him back and apologize. So, I told Julie we were going to go to the telephone store in the mall and buy a new phone. When we got to the mall, Julie went into the store to buy us a new phone.

While she did that, I went to a pay phone and called Congressman Brinkley. He had been waiting for my call.

"How did your conversation go?" he asked me.

"Well, Congressman," I said, "To give you a hint, let me tell you that I am calling you from a pay phone in the mall outside a store in which Julie is buying us a new phone. I tore the one we had off the wall."

I can't remember what Congressman Brinkley said. But, I do remember feeling bad that I had let him down.

Two nights later on Sunday night, Congressman Brinkley called me at our house and asked me, in a very cordial way, if I could meet him in his office at six o'clock the next morning. I said, "Yes, sir."

When I got off the phone, I was in a good mood. I told Julie that I would be going in to work early the next morning. I thought I had been doing a good job. I said, "He must be going to give me a raise, because nobody would ask you to come to work so early just to get mad with you."

The next morning, I got to the office before six o'clock. Congressman Brinkley was already there. At about 6:15, he called me and asked me to "join him" in his office. I went right in.

He told me to sit down on the big leather sofa that ran along one wall of his office. He had a stack of index cards in his hand. He said that he had thought about the trouble I had talking with that man on Friday. He said that I had not handled that telephone call very well.

Congressman Brinkley said that he had typed out some suggestions for how I could improve my handling of phone calls on index cards. He said that he had asked me to come to work early so that he would have time to go over them with me.

By this point, I had begun to doubt that I was going to be getting a raise. He took out the first index card and started explaining his first suggestion for how I could improve my telephone skills.

But, before he could finish making his point, he began scratching behind his ear with the stack of index cards he had in his hand. Before long, he was scratching all over his ears and head with the index cards.

The more he scratched, the more he itched. The itching was also spreading to other parts of his body. It was only 6:30 in the morning. Nobody else was in the office, and I had no idea what was wrong with him or what to do to help him.

He continued to try to talk to me about how to act on the telephone as he continued to scratch himself all over his body. I was worried there was something really wrong with him. Finally his secretary arrived.

He immediately called her into his office. She took one look at him and became very alarmed by all his scratching. She said, "Congressman, do you want me to call the House Physician's Office?"

He looked at her with blood shot eyes and said, "No. I want you to go to the drug store!" She asked, "What for?" He said, "Flea powder!"

It turned out that the previous week Congressman Brinkley's wife had come from the Brinkley's home in Columbus, Georgia, and spent the week with him at his condominium in a Washington suburb.

She had brought her two cats with her. On Friday, Congressman Brinkley had driven Mrs. Brinkley and her cats back to Columbus, and on

Sunday he had driven himself from Columbus back to Washington.

As he was sleeping Sunday night, the fleas that Mrs. Brinkley's cats had left in his condominium had gotten in his hair. He had not known anything about it until he started giving me lessons on how to talk on the telephone.

When his secretary returned from the drug store, he had about had it. He just took the index cards he had in his hands and gave them to me. Then, he looked at his secretary and me and said, "Don't tell anybody I have fleas!"

# CHAPTER 33

## The Subway Caper

Congressman Brinkley was a very dignified and intelligent man. But he had so many responsibilities that it would have been impossible for him to stay on top of everything going on in both the district and Washington.

He did very important work for our country every day, and I was honored to help him. But, those things are harder to remember than the amusing things that were bound to happen from time to time. After all, the people who get elected to lead our nation do not stop being human just because they get sworn into office.

This story illustrates that point. It is something Congressman Brinkley and I both laughed about when it was over.

One Monday, Congressman Brinkley called me from Columbus. He told me that he was going to fly into National Airport the next morning. He told me he had never taken the subway from the airport to the Capitol before, and he asked me if I was familiar with how it worked. I told him that I was. So, he asked me to meet him when his plane landed and show him how to get from the airport to the Capitol on the subway.

The next morning, I met his flight and escorted him to where you get on the subway at the airport. When we got on the subway car, we sat down. At that point, the subway was above ground, but I knew that in just seconds after it left the airport, it would travel underground all the way to the Capitol.

The other people on the subway recognized that he was a Congressman, and they became quiet. When we sat down in the subway, I had taken the seat beside the window, leaving Congressman Brinkley in the seat beside me on the aisle.

The first thing he said was that he wanted to change seats with me. He said, "I've never been on this subway before, and I'd like to sit by the window." The other passengers heard this and broke into laughter. They knew that five seconds after the subway left the station, there would not be anything to see but total blackness. Congressman Brinkley had no idea why they were laughing, and I didn't want to tell him. A few seconds later, he figured it out.

The first stop that subway made was at the Arlington National Cemetery exit. When the subway stopped, Congressman Brinkley got up and said, "That was the quickest I ever went from the airport to the Capitol." Again, the other passengers cackled with laughter.

I said, "Congressman, this isn't the Capitol. This is the exit for the Arlington National Cemetery." "Oh," he said, "When we voted to build this subway, I thought it was going to go nonstop from the airport to the Capitol so Congressmen could get to their offices quicker."

I told him that there would be several more stops before the subway got to the Capitol. He looked a little frustrated to hear that he wasn't going to be whisked non-stop from the airport to the Capitol.

When we finally got to the Capitol exit and got off, he looked around. "Where is the Capitol?" he asked me. I pointed to it and said, "Right over there, Congressman."

He said, "You mean this won't take us under our office building?" I said, "No, sir."

As we walked to the Rayburn House Office Building, he said, "I thought this connected with the subway system under the Capitol that we use every day." I said, "No, sir. I wish it did."

I don't think he ever took that subway again. After all, cars were quicker, you could park them right under the Rayburn office building, and they gave their passengers a much better view.

# CHAPTER 34

## Sights and Sounds

I have always loved history, so having the privilege of working for Congressman Brinkley in Washington was a dream come true for me. Every day, I got to go to the Capitol building as part of my job. Most days at lunch, I would walk through the pedestrian tunnel under our office building all the way to The Library of Congress.

When the tunnel ended and I walked up to the sidewalk, I was almost right across the street from The United States Supreme Court Building. At that point, I walked a little further to a drug store that had a large collection of newspapers and magazines for sale.

From the window beside my desk, I could look out on a hidden part of the roof of the Capitol building.

There were always two or three Capitol workers on that roof.

They had an interesting job. They would take American flags out of boxes and hoist them up and down a short flag pole, which could not be seen from the ground. It seemed like they did this all day long. Each flag stayed on top of that flag pole for less than ten seconds. Then, it would be replaced by another flag just like it. It seemed to me that these flags were being raised and lowered on that secluded flag pole every time I looked out my window.

After it was lowered, each flag was put in an individual box with a certificate saying that on that date that particular flag had flown over The United States Capitol. Of all the gifts that members of Congress were allowed to give to constituents, these flags were the most prized.

When constituents received one of these flags and read the certificate, they may have thought that the flag they were sent had flown on the main flag pole of the Capitol for an entire day. Well, even though that wasn't quite the case, the flags had all flown in the rarified air above the U. S. Capitol, so they were truly special.

In addition to all the historic places I got to be around every day, I also got to be around some very famous people. It was almost impossible to walk down the hall or get on an elevator without seeing somebody I had seen on the news many times.

The Rayburn House Office Building is a 2,395,914 square foot structure. It contains office suites for 169 Members of Congress, in addition to rooms for various Congressional committees and subcommittees.

The first day I worked there, I was walking around the maze of hallways looking for the office of another Member of Congress to whom Congressman Brinkley had asked me to deliver an envelope.

When I looked at the entrance to the office of a Member of Congress, all I could see was a receptionist sitting behind a desk. I noticed that these receptionists were some of the most beautiful women I had even seen in my life.

It would have been hard for me not to look at such beautiful women. I had just passed the most beautiful receptionist I had seen so far, when the large clocks that hung on all the walls up and down the halls of the building started flashing and making a loud ringing sound.

Thinking back to the controversy President Carter got into during the 1976 campaign, when he answered a question in an interview in *Playboy* magazine by admitting that he had lusted in his heart, I thought, "Oh, my gosh! They've installed a lust detector, and I've been caught!" I was really expecting a Capitol police officer to come along and take me away.

When I got back to our office, Congressman Brinkley asked me if I had delivered the envelope. When I told him the story about being caught by the lust detector, he laughed about as hard as I ever saw him laugh. "Those clocks light up and those bells ring to let members know what is taking place on the House floor," he said.

I later found out what the flashing lights and ringing bells on those clocks meant. Two lights and two rings meant members had fifteen minutes to get to the House floor and vote. Three lights and three rings meant there was a quorum call. Four lights and four rings meant the House had adjourned. Five lights and five rings meant members had only five minutes to get to the House floor and vote. Six lights and six rings meant the House was in recess.

But, thankfully for me, there were no lust detectors in the building. In fact, if such things existed, Capitol Hill would probably have been the last place to install them. With those receptionists sitting in every doorway, they would have made way too much noise.

# CHAPTER 35

## An Interesting Visitor

One morning, Congressman Brinkley called me into his office. "We're about to have a very distinguished visitor," he told me.

He told me that Admiral Hyman G. Rickover had called and asked for a meeting with him. Congressman Brinkley said he had never met him before, but he had heard a lot about him.

He said he wanted me to join him in his meeting with the Admiral. He said that, when the meeting was over, he wanted me to go to my desk and write a detailed report of everything that was said in the meeting.

I had heard Jimmy Carter talk about Admiral Rickover. Carter had worked under Admiral

Rickover in the program that developed the first nuclear powered submarine. Admiral Rickover was a four star admiral who won many awards, including two Congressional Gold Medals and the Presidential Medal of Freedom. He served on active duty for 63 years, making him the longest-serving member of the U.S. armed forces in history. A Los Angeles-class submarine was named after him.

As the time for the meeting neared, Congressman Brinkley and I were in his office waiting for the Admiral. When the Congressman's secretary announced that the Admiral had arrived, we stood up to greet him.

When you entered Congressman Brinkley's private office, the first thing you saw was a large, thick, lush rug with the State Seal of The State of Georgia embroidered on it. The seal is made up of an arch with three columns symbolizing the constitution and the three branches of government. Around the columns are banners which read "Wisdom," "Justice," and "Moderation." There is also a soldier representing protection of the constitution standing and holding a drawn sword between two of the columns.

When Admiral Rickover entered Congressman Brinkley's office, he looked down at the seal on that rug. Then, he looked up and said, "Why do you have a rug with a picture of a filling station sewn onto it?"

That was just the beginning. The rest of the meeting was just a parade of similar questions from Admiral Rickover addressed to Congressman Brinkley. When Congressman Brinkley tried to answer a question, the Admiral would just interrupt him and move on to another question. There was never a hint of humor. He was dead serious about everything he said. The Admiral's questions went on for over an hour. Finally, he said that he had to go, and he left.

When Congressman Brinkley closed the door behind him, we both broke into laughter. "What do you think, Dugan?" he asked me.

"Well, Congressman, I think that man is either a genius or out of his mind, but I don't know which. I just know that I've never met anyone like him before." "That's what I think, too," Congressman Brinkley said.

Then, I went to my desk and wrote a full report of everything I could remember from the meeting. I went back to Congressman Brinkley's office and gave it to him. He read it, smiled, and said, "Thank you for writing this."

I don't know what happened to that report. I didn't keep a copy. I wonder as I write this if it is right now in one of the hundreds of boxes of Congressman

Brinkley's documents that are housed at Columbus State University. If it is, I would surely like to read it one day.

As fascinating as Admiral Rickover was, he wasn't the only historically prominent person who I met while working for Congressman Brinkley. One of former President Franklin Roosevelt's sons worked very closely with Congressman Brinkley to preserve and promote the historical significance of FDR's Little White House in Warm Springs, Georgia.

James Roosevelt and Congressman Brinkley worked together on this project. In 1980, this famous place was designated a National Historic Landmark by the Interior Department. Other members of Congressman Brinkley's staff worked very closely with Mr. Roosevelt on this matter.

I only got to meet him and talk with him briefly. But, that was long enough for me to know that, compared to Admiral Rickover, he seemed like "a regular guy."

# CHAPTER 36

## A Good Lesson

One morning, Congressman Brinkley asked me and another one of his staff members to join him in his office. He said that there was an important matter that he wanted us to work on that day.

He told my friend to prepare a press release about it, and he told me to write a letter about it.

We both worked hard on what he told us to do. When we finished, we put our work on his desk, so he could have it when he got back to the office that afternoon.

Late in the afternoon, he got back to the office from the House floor and read what we had prepared for him. Then he called us both into his office.

First, he picked up the letter I had written for him and tore it down the center. Then, he put the two halves of it together and tore them. Then, he swiveled around in his chair and dropped the remnants of my letter in his garbage can under the credenza behind his desk. "I just wanted you to see me do that," he said.

Next, he did the exact same thing with the press release that my friend had written. Then, he looked at us and told us to do better.

He looked at me and asked, "Can't you write a better letter than that?" I said, "No, sir, Congressman. I worked very hard on that letter. It's the best I can do. If you want somebody to write a better one, you better ask somebody else to do it, because that's the best I can do. If I could write a better letter, I would have already done it."

He didn't seem too pleased with my answer. Then, he asked my friend, "Can't you write a better press release than that?" My friend said, "Oh, yes, sir. I didn't think that one was very good, myself. I'll write a better one right now."

This exasperated Congressman Brinkley. He said, "You mean that you brought me a press release that you didn't even think was very good? Why would you do that? At least he thought his letter was the very best that he could do!"

I don't remember what happened after that. I just have always remembered that lesson. It taught me a lesson that I have followed ever since. If you have a job to do, do it the very best you can and stand behind it. You might not be able to convince anybody else that you did a good job, but at least they will know that you did the very best you could. And, when people believe that, they don't stay mad with you very long and they at least respect your effort.

I have learned that one of the greatest benefits of working for great people is the lessons you learn from just being around them. I certainly learned a lot of lessons from Congressman Brinkley that I have never forgotten.

But, he learned a lesson from me one time, too. He told me about this himself.

A large civic club in Columbus invited me to make a luncheon speech. After I made my speech, they gave me a long standing ovation.

About a month later, Congressman Brinkley made a speech to the same club. When he finished his talk, he got a polite round of applause, but no standing ovation.

Congressman Brinkley told me that he asked a friend of his who was in the club why I got a standing ovation and he just got some polite applause.

"Oh, Jack," he told me his friend said, "don't you see? When you showed up, you looked so dignified and confident. We knew you would make a good speech, and we were looking forward to hearing you.

"But, when this Dugan guy was sitting at the head table, he looked so nervous. He couldn't eat anything and his hands were shaking so much that he could barely hold his glass of water without spilling it.

"So, we were expecting to have to sit through a horrible ordeal of a talk. When he made a good talk, we were so relieved and happily surprised that we gave him a standing ovation. We felt like we had dodged a bullet."

Congressman Brinkley said I had a big advantage because people did not expect as good of a speech from me as they did from him. He said the lesson he learned was that people react to what you do based on whether it is better than what they were expecting as much as on how it compares to what other people might be able to do.

I always remembered that lesson, too. In speaking to people, I try to start slow and improve as I go along. Reducing people's expectations is a good way to take the pressure off yourself, and it can make you seem better than you are.

# CHAPTER 37

## A True Friend

One Thursday or Friday in early 1982, Congressman Brinkley asked me to have lunch with him in the Members' Dining Room in the Capitol. It was an election year, and Congressman Brinkley had something specific that he wanted me to do for him.

I don't remember the exact details of why, but he asked me to play the role of a possible opponent and debate issues that might come up in the 1982 election with him. We had a good time doing that.

As we made our way back from the Capitol to Congressman Brinkley's office in the Rayburn building, we had a good time. If there was anything bothering him, I didn't sense it.

He went home to Columbus that night. Since he had asked me to debate issues with him that could come up during the campaign year, I had no doubt that he was going to run for reelection. I also knew that nobody would have a chance to beat him.

The following Monday morning when I got to work, Congressman Brinkley called the staff from Columbus. He told us that he had decided not to run for reelection that year. After he finished talking to us all, he asked me to go into his office. He said there was something he wanted to talk with me about in private.

When I went into his office and closed the door, I sat down at his desk and talked with him on his phone. I don't remember the entire conversation. I do remember that he asked me if I wanted to run for his seat in Congress that year.

I thought it was very kind of him to ask me, but I told him that I didn't want to do it. The main thing that went through my head when he asked me was that I didn't want him to think I had come back to work for him just because I wanted to try to succeed him. Considering how kind he had been to hire me back, I wanted to be sure that I was loyal to him.

Towards the middle of the year, Congressman Brinkley offered me the chance to move back to Columbus and work for the remainder of the year in his Columbus office. I was grateful to get the chance to move back to Georgia before the new school year began for our older son.

The main thing we did for the balance of the year was to organize his files and prepare them to be donated to Columbus College. I really don't remember much else about that time period.

Congressman Brinkley was a lawyer, and I was, too. Towards the end of the year, he asked me if I wanted to open a law practice with him after his term ended in January. That was what I had been hoping would happen. We actually practiced out of the building that had been his Congressional office in Columbus.

Congressman Brinkley's younger son, Fred, was a good friend and fishing buddy of mine. We used to go fishing many Friday afternoons and practically every Saturday.

I had a great time fishing with Fred. Since Congressman Brinkley had recently retired from Congress, he got many invitations from people all over the district to come fishing in their private ponds and lakes.

Congressman Brinkley would tell these people that he didn't want to go fishing at their private lakes, but that Fred and I would surely like to. As a result, Fred and I could go to a new pond every Saturday. We found out that the best ponds were owned by heart surgeons.

These busy doctors bought ponds and lakes, had them stocked and expertly cared for, but didn't have much time to fish. We used to laugh when it seemed like the big bass in these well maintained ponds had never seen a plastic worm before. Those were very good times.

During his time in Congress, Jack Brinkley did a great job for the people in his district. He protected and enhanced the stature of the district's two big military installations, Fort Benning and Robins Air Force Base. He also got Columbus connected to the Interstate Highway System, among many other accomplishments.

His greatest accomplishment, in my opinion, was a lot less noticeable. He helped thousands of constituents get through difficulties they encountered working with agencies of the federal government. These private struggles people had dealing with the bureaucracy were more impactful to their lives than any political issue ever could have been.

Congressman Brinkley did not get rich or famous from politics, compared to many other politicians. He also didn't stay in Washington as a high paid lobbyist, like so many others did.

He really did never forget who he was, where he was from, or who sent him. When we started practicing law together, lots of people who had helped him in his campaigns came to him for their legal needs. He kept his integrity and earned people's trust.

Years later, after I became extremely depressed, Julie and I were in a dire situation. We had one very old car, but it quit working. Congressman Brinkley heard about this and called me. He said he wanted to lend me his car for us to use. I don't know how we would have made it without his help.

Not long before he died, it just popped into my head that I should call him. We were living in Mobile, Alabama at the time. I'm so thankful to God that I did. His voice was very strong. He was extremely kind in what he said to me. I told him how much I appreciated everything he had done for me. Then, I told him that I loved him.

That was the last time I ever talked with Jack Brinkley. It was a perfect conclusion to a wonderful friendship.

# CHAPTER 38

## Carter and Brinkley

When I woke up on Saturday morning, March 5, 1966, I had no idea that God was going to set the course for the entire remainder of my life by what He would cause to happen before I went back to bed that night. It is truly unbelievable.

That night, God caused me to meet two very great men, Jimmy Carter and Jack Brinkley. They both had such a huge impact on my life that I simply have no idea what my life would have been like if I had not met them.

I hope I have conveyed to you a picture of what wonderful people they both were. I hope God has helped me to share the human side of both of them. This is my tribute to them.

I'm convinced that they both loved me, and I know that I loved them. I am so proud of them for the people they were and so thankful to God that his plan for my life included allowing me to be their friend.

They were both from very small Georgia towns. Everybody knows that Jimmy Carter was from Plains.

As for Congressman Brinkley, I heard him begin hundreds of speeches by saying that he was born in Faceville, Georgia. Then, he would grin and add, "It's a little town right between Climax and Recovery." Sure enough, it is. I have found all three of these towns on the map.

Both Carter and Brinkley believed in serving their country. Jimmy Carter was a submariner and Jack Brinkley was an Air Force pilot. I used to travel with him a lot in his car. He had a very big compass installed on top of his dashboard. I asked him what it was one day. He said, "This is the compass I had on my airplane when I was in the Air Force."

Both Jimmy Carter and Jack Brinkley believed in treating all people equally. I never even one time heard either one of them say, do or even condone anything at all that could be considered racist or discriminatory.

They were both tough and wise. They were both guided by high standards of integrity and hard work.

They were both devoted to their friends. When I practiced law with Congressman Brinkley, we had meetings every Monday to see where we stood financially. We never stood very well off financially.

It wasn't because we didn't have clients. People flocked in to see Congressman Brinkley. The problem was that they had all helped him in his campaigns. So, he had a hard time charging them a realistic fee.

I remember one time he worked practically an entire week preparing a will for a kind woman who had been one of his first supporters.

At our meeting the next Monday, he said he had finished her case and that she had paid him in full. Then, he handed me the check she had written. It was for exactly ten dollars.

Congressman Brinkley beamed. He said, "Look what she wrote on it." In the bottom left hand corner where the check had the word "for" followed by a blank line, she had filled in, "A loving service."

They were both Christian men. They knew the Bible from cover to cover. They quoted it and they were guided by it.

They were big enough to handle the toughest challenges, and yet humble enough to do the smallest things. When I worked for Congressman Brinkley in Washington, he demonstrated this in a special way.

Whenever a constituent came to visit him with his family, I watched to see if there were any young children in the group. If there were, I knew what was coming next.

The light on my phone that was reserved for Congressman Brinkley to call me would light up. I would answer it. He would say, "Will you join me, and please bring me my potato."

By potato, he meant everything he needed to perform his magic tricks. I would go to a storage closet, get down the "magic box," and take it into him. He would then use his toothpicks, his potato, and a glass of water to perform a magic trick for the constituent's children.

I watched him perform his magic tricks many times, but I never understood them. I just didn't see what was magic about them. But, I understood one thing. Those constituents were very important to him.

When a page came to work for a few months, Congressman Brinkley always had the entire staff assemble on the Friday before they left to go back to Georgia for a going away party.

The highlight of these parties would come when Congressman Brinkley read a poem he had composed for the person who was going back to Georgia. The poems were not too remarkable, but the feeling behind them was.

When he finished reading the poem, which his secretary would have typed for him on his thickest Congressional stationary, he would sign it and hand it to the recipient while announcing, "This is a Brinkley original!"

If somebody did something good, he would tell them, "You have just become a member of the Brinkley hall of fame." When he had to leave a group of constituents at the end of a speech, he would say, "Now I must leave, for I have miles to go and promises to keep. Tomorrow, at this time I shall be in the people's house."

I am notorious for talking too long. Congressman Brinkley's way of handing this was to tell me, "Dugan, during this conversation, let's invoke the five minute rule," referring to House procedure.

When I left Washington to move back to Georgia, he called me into his office and gave me his copy of the Congressional Bible. It is a 1,104 page long book given to members of Congress that contains the Constitution, Jefferson's Manual, and Rules and Practice of The House of Representatives.

On the inside cover, he had written:

"July 16, 1981

"To my friend Steve Dugan, Counselor and Legislative Assistant.

"Jack Brinkley, M.C.

"Washington, D.C."

It is one of my most treasured possessions. I am looking at it right now. It almost makes me cry.

Time goes by so quickly. I thank God that he allowed my time to intersect with the time of Jimmy Carter and Jack Brinkley.

The last thing I will say is this. I knew both Jimmy Carter and Jack Brinkley very well. I saw them in good times and in bad times.

I saw their public sides and their human sides, and I love them both. I know that if you had the opportunity to know them as I did, you would have loved them, too.

Printed in the United States
by Baker & Taylor Publisher Services